OUT OF THE WRECKAGE

Allan Kolski Horwitz

Dream Parables

Botsotso Publishing

PUBLISHED IN 2008 BY BOTSOTSO PUBLISHING
BOX 30952, BRAAMFONTEIN, 2017
EMAIL: botsoso@artslink.co.za
WEBSITE: www.botsoso.org.za

ISBN

978-0-9814068-2-4

WE WOULD LIKE TO THANK THE NATIONAL LOTTERY DEVELOPMENT
TRUST FUND FOR ITS SUPPORT.

ACKNOWLEDGEMENTS

Some of these stories have been previously published in the following anthologies,
magazines and websites: Botsotso Manuscript Exhibition 1, Green Dragon,
In the Rapids, Litnet, Mad Hatter's Review, New Contrast, Ons Klyntji,
Unity in Flight, Viva Life,Viva Love.

COVER AND TEXT DESIGN
Katherine Finlay

CONTENTS

Sometimes the veil fades slowly
Sometimes the veil slips
Sometimes the veil is ripped
in one motion

A wave forms
swells
reaches its high point
then breaking
is followed by a lull
-a windy or calm surface

Slowly
the new tide rises

A young man catches a fish
a small fish
He laughs excitedly
throws it back into the ocean
-it is too small to eat
or tosses it into a can
to be used as bait

He still dreams of a big fish

Sometimes the veil yields to another veil
Sometimes the veil itself decides to unveil
Sometimes we cannot believe the veil
is a veil

Sometimes the veil is so beautiful
we insist on it

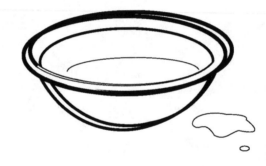

THE PRESIDENT

After many years of unchallenged power, the President - intermittently, haltingly, often incoherently - begins to question himself; begins to examine his tribe's relationship with other tribes in their country. Particularly the ones who had opposed him at the start of his rule; the ones who had resisted his coup and organized demonstrations in the capital, and when their protests had failed to persuade him to respect the election results, had caused diplomatic petitions to be circulated all over the continent, and forced the United Nations to pass resolutions of censure. But he had stood firm, called their bluff. And when these resolutions were shown to be ineffectual (they had not moved him to renounce his illegal action in favour of the elected candidate who was from another tribe, nor motivated him to hold fresh 'free and fair' elections), these other tribes had taken up arms and challenged his army. And though their rebellion had been well supported, so much so that the country was effectively partitioned, he had not shrunk from pacifying them, leading to months of all out war when nothing seemed to work except the methods that in his youth he had attacked the old imperial powers and the corrupt military juntas of other countries for using . . .

But now, thirty years down the line, all those ancient doings should have been entirely washed under his belt, and under the splendid new bridge built over the brown river on whose banks the old colonial city had been hacked out of the jungle (the stylish and imposing bridge designed by a new generation of engineers from the old empire which had been - as was to have been expected - named after him by the Party). For now, of course, the President is absolutely entrenched and opposition to his rule is a figment of memory, a fiction.

And the President, like all his subjects, cannot truly recall that time so that these reflections (on the manner of his having come to power and the resultant abuses) occur in a disorganized, rambling manner, generally when he is alone, often in the early hours when indigestion has forced him awake, or his wife (or the mistress he has chosen for that night) has unknowingly rolled onto him, breaking his sleep. Ah, sleep, always precarious . . . How can presidents easily close their eyes and slip into dreams? So it is that these thoughts of his corruption gnaw away at him in a desultory and fanciful way given the great odds against remembering, given the obstinate and obtuse historical haze.

Then one afternoon, while a servant is wheeling in a trolley with delicacies, and he, in his capacity as governor of the Central Bank, is about to sign a report on the economic prospects for the coming quarter (a report prepared by a foreign expert on behalf of a multi-national corporation interested in 'developing' various mineral resources), rationalizations and denial can no longer sustain him. He admits to himself that for thirty years he and his tribe have exploited the defeated, seized their land, displaced them from the civil service, shut them out of schools and universities and forced them into the most menial, low paying jobs.

And from this day, though the President sits at his desk appearing affable and collected, he is possessed by guilt and remorse. How could he have betrayed the ideals of his youth, the very motives that had pushed him into political struggle: the vision of justice? And the inner conflict causes him to gradually lose composure, so that his control of the country wavers, as does his ability to tolerate those around him. For each day he has to witness (and stomach) the arrogance and duplicity of his fellow tribal politicians, generals, government officials and businessmen; all of them, none less than himself, having handsomely benefited by wielding the levers of patronage. He has to sit in meetings and banquets, receptions and other ceremonies, laughing and conniving with them. And then, once the nerve-wracking day is over, he has to face the night.

Every night he dreams he is in a hospital. And there in that hospital he ministers to the downtrodden and diseased of the most oppressed tribe. He washes and cleans their sick and destitute, empties their bedpans, patiently feeds them when they are too weak to do so themselves, sings lullabies to comfort their dying children. Night after night he makes amends for his past crimes and those of his tribe. But every morning, instead of waking refreshed and purified by these acts of piety and contrition, he feels more unsettled. And sitting up in his capacious bed, still warm and languid, sated on the voluptuous woman beside him, blinking in the well tempered light of his luxurious bedroom, he struggles to admit that the reason for his discomfort is seemingly trivial, and yet so humiliating. For every night the dream ends with the same climax: In the bed at the end of the ward, near the door that leads out onto a scummy red concrete stoep, lies an old woman who refuses to allow him to touch her. He wants to serve her, to wash and perfume her, but every night she spurns him. And her scream, warning him to stay away, shocks him awake; a jagged scream impregnated with insult that he can no longer bear so that he fears falling asleep.

Revolted by the behaviour of his tribespeople, wracked at night by the dying woman's rejection, the President sinks into depression. He becomes obsessed with his country's suffering: the disintegrating hospitals and schools, the potted roads and dilapidated buildings, the starving children in the urban slums. But he knows that to carry out the necessary changes will necessitate a dramatic upheaval - his past cronies will think him insane, and mock him. And should he have the audacity to challenge them, and hold them to account, they will rise up against him with the backing of the generals, one of whose number will be appointed the new leader once he is either killed or driven into exile.

Months pass, each more disturbing. But, finally, the President calls a special sitting of parliament (despite 'one party' rule the institution enjoys a certain status and is partially successfully in creating the illusion of democracy), and instructs the state media to report that an important proclamation is to be made. On the appointed day he arrives with the usual cavalcades and military parades. And once the assembled functionaries have eased back into their seats, he informs them of his annulment of all discriminatory and oppressive legislation (particularly those laws that have kept the other tribes' hostage) and announces that he is setting up a special fund to pay the wronged, reparations. And while the parliament sits in stunned silence, he adds that all political prisoners are to be freed and that he will summon a further special sitting to endorse a new constitution. His concluding statement is that new elections, to be supervised by the continental organization of unity, will be held within six months, and that as soon as the results have been ratified he intends to step down as president. Then he leaves the chamber and returns to his palace. Thereafter, when the news is broadcast, the country goes into shock.

The leaders of the oppressed tribes unreservedly hail him as a righteous man and grant him pardon for the crimes of the past, celebrations are held in all their towns and villages. The outside world, too, applauds; the international media file adulatory reports. But the President's tribal leaders, appalled by this abrupt and abject surrender of their privileges, condemn him as a traitor, and the army, expecting a purge once the new human rights respecting government is elected, begins to mobilize.

The President convenes another parliamentary session, praying that he will find allies while the process of implementing the planned election takes hold. But he is confronted by a united threat: step down immediately in favour of another tribal personality or face assassination. He looks beyond the ruling party but the other tribes have no strength; their organizations, long banned, cannot hope to mobilize support quickly enough. Then what of the broad masses of his own tribe? They have not benefited from nepotism to the same degree as the elite. Their lives are in most cases also blighted. Will they not welcome a new, more just form, of government? Surely they are his best hope? But how is he to gauge their feelings?

Dressed in casual, even shabby clothes, he leaves the presidential palace and wanders through the city, listens to the conversations of the streets and marketplaces, the taxi ranks, the football stadiums and the bars. The discussions are vociferous - his announcements have inflamed the country: he hears himself alternately congratulated and derided, but overall there is powerful endorsement and appreciation of his wisdom and courage. Almost in a trance, moving from one suburb to another, the President soaks up this direct, honest contact. And at night, reaching the outskirts of the city, he enters the most dangerous area - a shantytown, a settlement of the abandoned, those most ravaged by disease and hopelessness. He sits down with a group of men drinking cheap beer in a shack. They do not disappoint him – there is unanimous approval of his actions, toasts are raised to him, hope expressed for a sublime future.

Past midnight, now exhausted, but finally at peace, he lies down by the side of a road and falls asleep. And he dreams again of the hospital. But this time, not only the old, dying woman at the end of the ward will not accept him - none of the sick will allow him to touch them; they all now reject and taunt him. He wakes, shocked by this reversal. The dream is inexplicable, perverse. After all, he has taken the ultimate step, shown his repentance in the most direct and meaningful way, so much so that he is now a pariah in his own class and community. Why then in the dream is he still plagued by the consequences of evil, by unresolved historic injustice? And why is his rejection so complete that the symbolic if phantom sick, who so much need help, and who were formerly so appreciative of his efforts, now try to eject him from the hospital? Tens of sweaty hands clambering to push him out . . .

He lies awake for hours by the roadside, racked by incomprehension and a sense of betrayal, dogged by the fear that it is, in fact, impossible to achieve redemption. And then, while he lies in this dazed state, a young thug, of whom there are many in this shantytown, strikes him on the head, stabs him in the chest and steals his shirt, his shoes and the few coins he has in his pockets. The President cries out for help but people pass him by. What is he to do? He is weak from his wounds and cannot walk unaided. A day of agony passes. Then, at last, before sunset, a beggar, showing pity for his wretched condition, takes him to a nearby hospital.

At first the President is not identified. Distraught, haggard from lack of sleep, his face distorted by pain, he is, indeed, unrecognizable as the suave, if corpulent figure the world was accustomed to. The nurses admit him without comment and provide him with a small cot in the corner of a ward. But that night one of the patients recognizes him. The man is from his tribe and his reaction is one of great anger. He calls the other patients, demands of the nurses that the President be expelled from the hospital: he must pay for his treachery. The mob drags him from his cot.

The President shields his face, but their blows rain down mercilessly till a great cry rises up from a bed at the end of the ward.

"Leave him! He is a light! Leave him! Leave the just man!"

And the cry is so piercing, so urgent and forceful, that even as the enraged patients are about to deliver their last fatal hits, they back off.

The President looks up, touches his battered face. He is still alive! He staggers to his feet and approaches the bed from where the cry had come. A shapeless mass lies shrouded by a dirty sheet. A dry, wizened hand reaches out. He puts the hand to his lips and kisses it. The hand squeezes his, then slowly withdraws

"Thank you, thank you," he says, then adds, "Please, may I see your face. May I never forget who it was that saved me."

At first there is no response, but slowly the coarse fabric is lifted, and in the faint light he sees that his saviour is the dying woman from his dreams, she who had refused to let him touch her. He starts, overwhelmed with surprise and gratitude. And then, as he again stammers his thanks, though in agony herself, she rises from her bed, lifts a basin of water and begins to wash his wounds.

DISCOVER

P icture a narrow bay ringed by high cliffs.
On one side is a slope filled with villas. Glaring white walls
and red tiled roofs rise up in layers above tidal inlets massed with
plantations of seaweed. On the other side, cut midway into the white
chalk of the cliff, a solitary house made up of several bright, airy,
empty rooms and long balconies, hangs over the water. Below this
house, at the base of the cliff, is a conglomeration, a vast assemblage
of rocks; giant blocks lying one on top of the other in a jumble of
angles that merge with the water.

Two young men live in this house. Aries manages, organizes every-
thing; and Pisces performs the tasks he is set, for he reveres Aries. We
do not know how long they have lived together, nor whether they are
indeed kin, but their affection is open and spontaneous, their inti-
macy intense. And so, with Aries wrapped in Pisces's adoration and
obedience, they live in utmost harmony.

One day an old man appears on the rocks below the house. He is
white-haired and slightly stooped, but exudes great energy. He waves
to them. Leaning from a window, Aries and Pisces watch his gesturing
hands. He calls out that he has a gift for them, a gift of great beauty
and value. They are curious, intrigued by his offer, but without com-
menting to each other, present disinterested faces.

The morning stretches. The old man, showing great patience, con-
tinues to call out and wave. His booming voice repeats that the gift
is extraordinary, sure to delight and satisfy. He urges them to come
down to the rocks. Still Aries and Pisces show no outward reaction.
But then, having listened to his entreaties for a considerable time,
Aries becomes angry. Their lives are complete. Why this interference?

Deceiver! What can the old man offer? What is there that they do not already have?

So Aries rages, but he does not speak of this to Pisces. Instead, he withdraws to another room. And there, trapped between resentment and anger, he broods: the old man's gift will bring them harm, will destroy their peace and equilibrium. Outside the big bass voice still rings out, praising the quality of the gift that is ready. Aries feels increasingly pressured. But then, showing his familiar decisiveness, he prepares a sling. He carefully chooses a stone. Down below the old man continues waving, calling them down. Opening a window, Aries takes aim. He pulls back the sling, and with a great cry, releases it. The stone strikes the old man between the eyes. He falls into the water. Tangled in fields of seaweed, the old man's body is smashed against the rocks and is soon mutilated.

While this is taking place, Pisces hears loud cheering from above the house. He sees a group of young men and women have gathered at the top of the cliff. They shout out exuberantly - a boisterous, merry-making crowd. Then, one by one, they run down the cliff at great speed. On reaching the bottom, they explode in a wild dance, jumping about, leaping from boulder to boulder. Pisces stares at them. How carefree they seem! And as more and more run down the cliff, he feels a desperate need to join them. But what is he to do? Aries has disappeared. How can he secure permission?

The minutes drag by. Pisces is pushed to breaking point. Eventually, quite beside himself, he hurries out of the house, runs down to the rocks. At last, he will be part of the dancing throng! But when he approaches one of the boys, he is ignored. He tries to speak to one of the girls. At first a spark of friendliness crosses her face then she, too, moves off. Another girl dances near him, seems to invite contact, but before he can speak, she steps away. Pisces is bewildered. Why are these seemingly good-natured young people so hostile to him? He turns away, dejected. But as he begins to climb the rocks back up to the house, a third girl appears. Dressed in a white top, black tights rippling over her graceful, powerful legs, she strides towards him. Pisces is overcome with expectation – he imagines caressing her bare skin, her delicate freshness clinging to him. And when she jumps onto his back, he is overwhelmed.

He grips her legs, and filled with joy, begins jumping from rock to rock. She returns his embrace, melting into him passionately. He bounds about with even greater vigour. The sun above sparkles; the ocean glitters. Wrapped in her arms, feeling her breasts taut against his back, he is in an ecstasy. Then he sees the old man's bloody head floating in the water. He stops. How has this happened? What could have caused the death of the smiling white beard who had spoken so persuasively about a wonderful gift? The girl still presses him close; he feels her breath in his ear. But he is terror-stricken. What if she sees other parts of the old man's body floating among the islands of rotting vegetation? Mangled limbs wedged between the rocks. Will she blame him for this sordid reality, and be appalled? And he thinks to himself, "My love, I want to carry you forever. There should be no end! I must prevent your seeing this ghastly sight. For if you do, you will scream and leave me!"

Suspended - the girl perfectly nestled against him, her mouth hot against his neck, her hair draped over his eyes, her arms encompassing him - he watches the other young people still dancing about, wrapped in their youth and beauty. They do not see the old man's corpse.

There is no doubt as to what he must do.

He jumps into the swirling water.

A FARAWAY SHOPPING MALL

They had driven to a shopping mall in a faraway suburb to buy shoes. The selection had been enormous and the prices very low. They had bought several pairs and were well satisfied with their purchases.

In the parking lot, the son had unlocked the car. Then, before he could start the engine, his father had begun talking.

"You know, we were lucky today. We got good quality at great prices. Just shows - you got to check the ads. All sorts of good things come out of the ads. Son, we just got ourselves a couple of really great buys."

The son smiled. The Old Man wouldn't just buy trash for the sake of it. He had an eye for the tasteful. And even if on the rare occasions there was some extra cash in the bank, he stuck to his guns.

"Why overpay? What's the sense in that? So what if it takes a bit of tracking down, a bit of research, what's the harm in that? In any case, who wants to be taken for a sucker, ripped off, made a fool of by shysters? But we did well today. And you know something? This won't be the last time you see me here. This shop has got what it takes. Smart management. You can see it a mile away. These guys know that turnover is what counts in the shoe game. Unless you're going for the very top end, of course - the millio-bloody-naires. Us Joe Soaps want quality soles without paying an arm and a leg. We want good finishing without fancy trimming. Ja, my boy, we got lucky today." The father patted his son's arm. "Thanks for driving me. You've done your share today."

The son flushed. He was pleased to have satisfied his father. He loved his father and wanted be like him - independent, resourceful, one step ahead.

"We sure did, dad," he said. "But it wasn't just that we were lucky. You did your homework, dad. You must have phoned about fifteen stores to check the prices."

The father nodded. "Yup, I did my homework. You learning from that, boy?"

"Sure, dad. I'm listening, I'm watching. I know what to do. I seen you do it . . . plenty times."

"If there's one thing I want you to remember, it's this - don't get caught out. Don't let the bastards take you for a ride."

The boy nodded. "Ja, dad. No bastard's going to take me for a ride." Then they both turned, and looked appreciatively at the boxes of shoes on the backseat.

The old man blew his nose.

"Your mother . . . she never understood, never appreciated what I was doing - for her, for all of us. She never gave me my due. She never saw the need. Yes, my boy, she said I was crazy. Me, crazy? You know how much I saved us by doing my homework? Over the years, you know how many hours I spent, tracking down the shops in that old car we had. Hey, but that was a car! That was a beauty! None of the plastic crap we get today."

The father blew his nose again.

"She never gave a damn. Just wanted it all on her lap." He stuffed the tissue into his pocket. "Your ma, what can I say? May her memory be blessed . . . but when I think how she went on at me, how she wouldn't help with the bond . . . like she didn't understand, just wanted me to arrange everything like pulling rabbits from a hat, like it doesn't take any sweat, like it doesn't take homework. So what could I do? I sweated blood. Yes, son, I sweated blood and couldn't swallow food without a pain in the guts. The banks don't sleep. They come knocking at night. They wake you in the early hours and keep you up till dawn worrying about the end of the month."

The father shook his head.

"So we lost the house! The best house we ever had. You remember that view of the forest? You do? What a view! And now? What we got? A damn wall to stare at! Then, after that always onto to me, as if

I was a nothing."

The son said, "She couldn't work, dad, you know that. Mom was sick herself."

"Sick? Of course she was sick. Sick in the head! She could've worked from home. I was prepared to arrange everything. Telephone sales. I mean, that's money for jam. Policies or house selling. You can sit in bed and make calls and sweet talk the fools. Especially if you've got your mother's voice. Oh, she could be very sweet on the phone when she wanted something! Believe me, when she wanted something on the phone she got it. What she wanted. But she said it was beneath her to do sales. Said it was coarse. Can you believe such crap?"

The son started the car.

"I was sweating blood and she was playing Princess. Can you believe it? But she was a good mother to you boys. That I got to give her. She was a wonderful mother. Spoilt you rotten, of course, but gave a whole lot of love. A whole lot of love for you boys."

The son reversed the car out of the parking lot.

"No doubt about it, son. We got a bargain today."

THE DOG

A man and a woman sit facing each other. They are passengers in a carriage drawn by a team of fine, powerful horses. They are known to each other but keep a distance. Through the windows they see stars glittering in a frosty sky.

The carriage enters a dark wood. Perched in a tree that hangs over the rutted track, a robber lies in wait. When the carriage passes beneath him, he dives down and knocks the coachman to the ground. The reins fly into the air and the horses rear up, then surge forward. The carriage accelerates, the robber manages to seat himself in the coachman's place but he fails to retrieve the reins - they are thrown about or trodden under.

Tossing heads high, the team speeds unchecked into the darkness. Sparks scatter from the pounding hooves. And though a perfectly synchronized rhythm is maintained, the carriage begins to sway wildly. The man and woman lurch forward in their seats. They are aware that an accident, some violent upheaval, has taken place, but they cannot see the coachman's platform and do not know that the robber is on board. Hurtling through the forest, they become alarmed, frightened. But they adjust; and when no collision takes place, begin to relax, and at the same become aroused as the carriage seems airborne, and air rushes past in a caressing stream.

On and on, the horses gallop; sweeping along, out into open fields, back again into the forest. Effortlessly, yet with sweat streaming from their flanks, they keep up their breath-taking pace. Then, just before dawn, the carriage enters a small clearing in which stands a tower. Taken aback, the team slows down. And, as they falter, the robber is able to scoop down and sweep up the reins. He brings them to a stop. The man and the woman are surprised. The ride was surely dangerous - but such relief is secondary to their nightlong exhilaration. They peer out: the carriage stands motionless in front of a squat, conical, stone tower. The tower has a red tiled turret that rises to the level of the trees. At the base of the tower is a large black door studded with nails.

The man and woman alight from the carriage. The man strides up to the thick wooden door and pushes it open. He steps forward. Behind the door is another wooden door. This one, too, he pushes open. But each time he advances, there is another door. Again and again - door, after door, after door. Yet again he faces a black door studded with nails. He opens it.

Standing on the threshold is a growling, slavering dog with sharply pointed teeth.

The man plunges a knife into the beast's chest.

RED BEARD

A bel was raised in a small town. His family belonged to a religious sect that regulated every human activity and function: when and how and what to eat; what to wear; when and how and what to pray for - the words, expressions to be used for every situation; how men and women should interact; how children should be educated; what answers to give about the origin and meaning of our existence. However, when he was a young man, he left this highly disciplined sect (although it meant leaving his family whom he loved despite their intolerance, their narrow views tempered only sometimes by insight and compassion), and moved to a big city. And in the city he became active in a political organization that wished to radically change the values and structures of the wider society. Abel soon became one of the most militant cadres. Day after day, with unflinching commitment, he would rise at dawn to sell their newspaper, going from door to door to recruit new members. No task was too small or too petty for him, no person of such little consequence that he would not take the time and opportunity to educate. And though over-zealousness was a common failing of many of his comrades, Abel did not become bombastic or doctrinaire. Indeed, his openness and enthusiasm inspired many outsiders to join and strengthen the group.

A decade passed.

Organizational growth gave him a sense of achievement. But there were also frustrations. In particular, despite his superficial sense of community with the other activists, there were his unfulfilled relations with women. For Abel found that invariably, though for seemingly different reasons, his partners would leave. And this pattern - of infatuation, intimacy then dissolution - ran its course ten, eleven

23

times, till he became quite bitter, even cynical, about the chances of developing a true bond. So he would return late every night to an empty flat after hours of meetings and workshops, sit alone at the kitchen table, browse through the newspaper, heat a pre-cooked meal, then read a political tract before going to sleep. On the weekends there were also meetings, but he had a few hours for relaxation; for eating out, watching movies, going to the theatre or concerts, or playing sport - notwithstanding the fact that these ordinary activities can soften a revolutionary, can undermine focus and deflect energy away from the tasks at hand. In short, he had social contact but the deep love, the erotic, emotional and intellectual love between two people that reaches and sustains our roots, continued to elude him.

Then, one day, years after he had created his new life, Abel visited the town where he had grown up. He returned to his old neighbourhood, walked the familiar streets - from the family house to the shops, to the Temple, and then back again. He walked these too familiar streets and saw that nothing had changed. And he recalled how he had hated the time spent in the Temple: day by day forced to prostrate himself before the Holy Ark where the scrolls were kept - the scrolls written by the sacred Prophet whose every utterance was blessed by the Lord; forced to listen to the sermons, the prayers to the Prophet and to His Father, Lord God of Creation. Platitudes, sentimental invocations for relief - deluded thinking, not like the modern, fearless science his organization practiced. And if his organization also had its own Thinker, its own Ideologue whose writings they studied and emulated, discussed and applied, was that a fault? After all, this study was objective, rested on fact, on analysis, unlike the circular, self-serving arguments advanced by the sect's Council of Elders.

So it was that this visit to the town of his birth showed the rightness of his decision to leave; the absolute affirmation of this decision being a chance meeting with a girl he had liked during the last years of high school. Of course, nothing much had passed between them (in fact, boys and girls were strictly separated), yet in a covert and embarrassed way he had communicated his desire to her, and she had reciprocated with lowered eyes and blushes whenever they had met in the street or at the neighbourhood shop. Now he saw her again

24

outside the same shop, and she was pregnant and had four children in tow and was a greatly aged reflection of the beauty she had been. Moreover, her walking dutifully behind her husband (as demanded by the sect's tradition), appalled Abel. He had broken free of this narrowness - and not a moment too soon; his break, as difficult as it had been to survive the initial loneliness and confusion, was thoroughly vindicated.

Nevertheless, despite his shock and distaste at her servitude, her ugliness, he had smiled at her, and though she had not at first reacted, he had welcomed her abrupt glance, then discrete wave, once her husband was well ahead and the children looking elsewhere.

*

Another decade passed. Abel had become the deputy leader of the organization and its chief theoretician. On his way to a congress in another state, he chanced to again pass through his hometown. And this time when he strayed into his old neighbourhood, he was astounded to find a transformation that was both radical and overwhelmingly positive: the old cramped, twisted houses had been replaced by open boulevards flanked with imaginatively designed buildings; structures of every conceivable shape and dimension created the effect of multi-coloured sculptures surrounded by greenery and trees.

Over-awed and gratified, Abel wandered about soaking up the new atmosphere. Then he entered a complex of buildings that housed the main male seminary, a college for prospective preachers. And there, on the steps leading to the central campus, he found crowds of young men dressed in the customary black suits and hats of their elders. And these young men, in keeping with the cardinal rule for men of the sect, wore full, red beards. They talked to each other in animated, good-humoured spirit.

Abel was amazed. His memories - of hunched, under-fed, pale boys staggering silently under the weight of bags filled with archaic tomes - clashed with the palpable well-being of these youngsters. Their vivacity made a mockery of his past suffocation and subsequent revolt. Clearly this generation, though seeming to observe the Law as strictly as their fathers, was vigorous and attractive; their long traditional beards, silky, well trimmed, glowing. If only his generation had been able to live like this! So Abel watched the young men with a feeling of great satisfaction. And while he was doing so, a young woman dressed in modern urban wear (that immediately marked her as an outsider) ran into the courtyard of the seminary. Abel was surprised, but extremely pleased - if the guards, who had standing instructions to keep all women out of the seminary, had allowed her entry, this was truly a sign of great change.

She ran gracefully forward amongst the seminarians and Abel followed her, admiring her speed and sureness, confident that the young men would also applaud her. However, as she approached him, he was disturbed to see that she was crying and shouting out in a wild and rambling manner, and that the young men were turning away. Had she been hurt, violated? Was she calling out for help, for protection from attack? Abel listened carefully: no, she had not been attacked, though she was crying to be let in! She was crying out that this was her home - the seminary, the temple, the ritual bath, the tower, the braids, the wafer, the incense, the swaying! She was shouting out that she wanted to return and be accepted as she was, but the young men with their thick red beards were ignoring her.

Abel was astounded. How could they turn a blind eye to her? Why were they so hostile? Or was it that they could not, in fact, see her? Could not see her because she was unthinkable: this vibrant, independent young woman in the glory of her youth who wanted to return to her home, her community, but as an equal.

And watching her run towards them, he felt love for her. It was tragic that she could not have her wish. But what she wanted was not possible. Not yet. She would have to leave and wander elsewhere for some time before the Red Beards would welcome her. She would have to leave because her tears and cries could not, at this point, open their hearts or minds. And Abel also knew that he could not intervene and help her. The Red Beards were beyond him, too. So he left the town and did not see the young woman again although he dreamt of her for many years, and secretly prayed that he would one day meet her, and offer her his love, and be accepted by her. For surely she was the woman with whom he could unite in a holy communion?

THE TAP PLANT

Two boys plan a hike in the mountains. Their friends have thrown down a challenge: they must survive for seven days with supplies of food and water that would ordinarily suffice for one. To strangers, this dare may seem excessively daunting, but their friends know they relish such a trial, wishing for nothing more than to demonstrate their ability to adapt to natural conditions beyond the comforts of city life.

The boys pack basic equipment and the appropriately measured provisions. As a special concession, they take a cell phone for emergencies although it is understood that use of the phone will terminate the challenge. The mountains are familiar - they have hiked there many times - and despite a condition of the challenge being that they choose paths in areas that are particularly rugged, they feel confident. The only unknown factor is that of the water supply. Fortunately, though the summer has been a very hot one, there have been late rains, and they can reasonably expect to refill their bottles in the streams

On the day they set out, the sky is bright and blue. Their friends gather at the foot of a ravine that leads into the mountains. Toasts are raise to their success, everyone keyed up by the knowledge that it will be a difficult, testing experience. With final jokes and backslapping, the boys set off, and though the way is steep and they sweat, they soon leave the group of well-wishers behind. Drinking sparingly, they traverse a great ridge, progress across a second. At nightfall they camp out under the overhang of a giant rock. Enjoying a simple meal, warmed by a fire, chatting and laughing, they savour this first leg of their trial before falling asleep.

The second day is hotter than the first. By noon their water supplies have dropped by half, but taking careful note, they remain in high spirits. It is only when the sun begins to set, and they choose a new route that runs through a dense forest, that, fit as they are, this final stretch exhausts them. And that night, stretched out in their sleeping bags under the treetops and the stars, the first worry sets in: the few streams they had passed during these past two days have all been dry. Where they had hoped for gushing clear mountain water, they had only found sand and cracked rocks. But they do not panic. Eying the half-full water bottles (during the day dangling from the sides of their backpacks, now motionless beside them on the ground), they weigh up routes and evaluate which plants might, if faced with no other alternative, be sources of liquid - edible, non-toxic plants that contain significant quantities of sap and moisture.

At dawn they start out in the cool, but sharp inclines and steep passes force them to sip far too frequently than their reserve allows. Well before noon they rest under a large tree, for they dare not drink more. Only in the late afternoon, when the heat has subsided, do they crest another ridge. The pace is telling, the effort has been great. And that night a great fatigue attacks them. Aching muscles and a dull hammering in the head follow. Food, thus far rationed with great restraint, begins to taste foul. Even the greatly loved nightly fire seems ordinary, the stars mere pinpricks offering neither beauty nor fascination.

The fourth day takes them onto a dusty plain that links two sets of mountains. The powdery sand clings to and blocks their nostrils, ingrains itself on their lips, causes their legs to cramp. Soon, reaching the far foothills and deciding to camp, it is bitter to face their almost empty bottles, and still no river presents itself - just dry, stony, sandy grooves where floodwaters had once, aeons ago, etched out helter-skelter paths. They collapse under an enormous tree with barely enough strength to spread their sleeping bags. What are they to do in the morning? Turn back and weather their challengers' chiding - not to speak of their own cutting disappointment? To admit defeat after just four days would be an intolerably poor result! Or do they push on, and hope that water is to be found - around the next bend, over the following peak . . . ? The dustbowl has been overwhelming, the heat oppressive. They have difficulty in falling asleep, but still they good-naturedly take turns telling stories so as to relax and compose themselves for the crucial decision that must be taken by dawn.

With the first stirring of birds, morning comes dewless, dry as the previous days. But when they rise, there is no hesitation. They walk deeper into the mountains. And swearing to stretch out the hike for at least another week, they whistle defiantly. They make good progress. The glory of the day intoxicates them. They feel invincible. But after several hours, exhausted by the effort of crossing a very rocky terrain, they drain the last drops of water. They do so seated on a ledge overlooking a vast valley. The vista is grand, uplifting, but holding the empty bottles they have to face the unthinkable: how are they to reach the far end, or, for that matter, walk back to their starting point? Then one of the boys points to a cactus growing on the ledge. He pronounces its fleshy leaves water-bearing. The other disagrees, but the first is insistent. He breaks off a leaf and sucks the liquid spilling from the tear. The taste is bitter though his parched lips and throat rejoice. He mashes more of the leaves in his hand and sucks greedily. How revived he feels! He laughs at his companion's reluctance, teases him. He eats another leaf, and another. With each one his body seems to expand and his vision intensifies so that it seems he can see the minute veins in the cactus pulsate. He jumps up and down in awe and elation. And his companion also twists off a leaf and chews on it; and he too, is amazed at its sudden injection of energy. Truly this cactus has magical powers! Their thirst slaked, their bodies full and restored, they begin to laugh. How easy everything will be! The cactus is to found in abundance; but to be on the safe side, they will cut off enough leaves to last them for several days. Now they are sure to win the challenge!

But that night one of the boys has a dream: the cactus they have eaten is poisonous, if they do not purge themselves with water they will die. Sweating with fright, he wakes in alarm. His friend is fast asleep, breathing normally. Is this nightmare to be ignored? He falls back asleep, and this time he dreams that his friend is vomiting and crying, but that near them in the red sand, under a large black rock, is a plant that makes water - a tap plant. He wakes his friend. There are many large black rocks around them. But which covers the tap plant? They heave at the smallest boulder, and succeed in pushing it over. But there is no tap plant beneath it - no trace of water. They roll over another, and another, and another, but are disappointed. After overturning several more they are utterly exhausted and the dreaded decision has made itself - they must use the cell phone and accept defeat. But before they can bring themselves to do so, they both collapse. And stretched out, feverish, the dreamer sees a tap plant under a red rock - not a black one. They must find the strength for a final effort, a last superhuman burst!

The boy staggers to his feet. Indeed, there is a red rock near their sleeping place. They approach and push it, but the rock stays fixed, suspended over them - a stone delicately holding it in place. One of them kneels and slashes at it with his knife. The rock sways; he jumps clear as it rolls away. And there, where it stood, glowing in a sheath of green, they see a luxuriant fleshy brown plant, liquid drops cascading from the petals of its flowers. Their faith has been vindicated! It will counter the cactus poison and restore their strength! Soon they will fill their bottles and trek on. The drip of water in their ears, the exhortations of their friends wanting their lives to be victorious: all these sounds mingle as they drink their fill and then push on, deeper and deeper into the uncharted, no longer daunting mountains.

*

Several days later the search party finds them. Fortunately they are still alive. Both are lying in the shadow of a giant red rock. A stream runs just a little further on, its source under the red rock where it feeds the sacred cactus long known to ancient tribes as God's most potent but deadly hallucinogen.

BROWN BABY

It is an overcast autumn day.

I am in a studio. All around me are half-finished paintings. In the middle of the room, on a wide table that was once a door, lies an inert, ungainly, misshapen, pinky/gray baby. The baby is made of clay. I notice a piece of black cloth (or is it some other material?) embedded in the baby's navel. It gives off a foul smell. I begin to prize out the dark, string-like, wispy material and as I do so, a muddy looking substance gushes out, and I am so shocked by the unstoppable streaming of this substance, the sensation of disquiet and unease that touching it brings me, that I faint.

*

It is a sunny day in spring.

I am part of a group of men. We are gathered round a table. On the table, lying on his back, is a joyous, lustrous, brown baby boy. He gurgles. The baby looks at me very directly, very knowingly, and I wonder, with surprise, if I am his father. And I am overjoyed at the prospect, but also uncertain. Can I really be the father of this glowing, brown boy whose bright eyes, long limbs and fine features project such health, intelligence and beauty? Could I have created such a perfect child? I linger at the side of the table, unsure what to do. And this doubt paralyzes me - I am too scared to touch the baby or in any way acknowledge him.

But, then, looking at the men, some of whom I know and are my friends, and others who are not known to me but who seem open and approachable, I am reassured. For without even asking their opinion, everyone in the group smiles at me, nodding their heads, making it clear that they regard me as the father. And I bask in this recognition that is so immediate, unconditional, unforced. I return their smiles. Then I reflect that this is a doubly unexpected confirmation: for, notwithstanding their saluting me and my magnificent son, how can it be that they are unaware of my feelings of inadequacy - as a person, as a father - and that I cannot deal with my life? So we stand round the table; the men showing unfettered recognition of my having fathered the child, and I, freed of my doubts, pouring out my love for the baby.

He kicks his legs, clasps and unclasps his little hands. What a zestful boy! I fondle his cheek. But then, to my alarm, I see that he must be very uncomfortable - his head has been awkwardly propped against a piece of rough wood and his chin digs sharply into his chest. I am greatly angered by this discovery. How could the person responsible for placing him in this positon have been so unaware of the uncomfortable angle, and ignored his pain? But then, just as I am about to lift his head, and reposition it, he looks up at me, and despite his twisted neck, gurgles with happiness. I am amazed. This is even more astounding! That he should bear suffering with dignity at such a young age, and turn pain into laughter, is truly remarkable. The baby confidently reaches for my finger. And then, much as I am filled with satisfaction at his turning to me to spare him from distress, the old fear returns. Surely he cannot be my child? I am far too reserved and cowardly!

His head is now dangling dangerously, and he struggles to draw my finger to his mouth, but he does not give up and eventually suckles it. Again I rejoice. Such fortitude! I pick up the baby, embrace him; feel his heart beat against my chest. The men crowd around, their beaming faces showering me with congratulations. Then I lay the baby back on the table, this time placing his head in a more natural position. He settles comfortably, and gives me a splendid smile. I feel relieved. Placing his head in a more natural position did after all make a difference. However, after a few minutes, a frown clouding his features, he suddenly knocks his head from side to side at high speed like a programmed mechanical doll, and breathing convulsively, begins to cry.

We are all very alarmed. How can I reassure him, calm him? The crying grows louder. His legs shoot up, pummeling the air. The gathered men are silent. What could have so pained or frightened the good-tempered boy? Instinctively I bend over the table, outstretched arms ready to lift him. And as soon as he is able to see me, he stops crying. I quickly gather him and sway, lull him till his breathing steadies. Then I lay him down again. But this time, I place his head in the old, seemingly awkward position.

Immediately he offers a brilliant smile and gurgles, confounding my original indignation at this angling of his head. And I consider the possibility that the intention was in fact positive, almost praiseworthy - to enable the boy to observe his surroundings it was imperative to prop him up. Indeed, without placing his head at such an angle, he would not have been able to observe the group of men standing round him, and that would have included me! And I wonder about the identity of the responsible but mysterious person. What was his or her relationship to the bubbling little boy? Was it his mother? Then, still a little put out by my ignorance of who had played such an important role before me, I realize that at least now I have restored his view of the world and given back his sense of security, and there can be no further doubt about my being his father. So I smile to myself, and the men also smile, nodding their heads in satisfaction.

What a perfect spring day!

GERHARD

He wanted an ice cream. But the ice cream was on the other side of the street. He could hear the ice cream man shouting, "Ice cream, ice cream! Lollies, lovely lollies!"

"Ma, I want an an ice cream!"

She kept walking. The pavement was crowded. He tried again, but she moved forward, pushing the pram, ignoring him. Was it that she heard his voice but didn't want to understand the words? Usually she loved to watch him slurp and suck. But after the first one, "Ma," he would have said, "that was lekker. I want another one?" And, after that one, another one, now and tomorrow. And the next day. No, it wasn't that she was begrudging him, denying him.

Gerhard's ma was thirty-four. She didn't stand for people putting her down. She hadn't allowed Gerhard's father to do that

"Get the hell out of here. Get out now and take your fucking things!"

"OK, don't shout."

Gerhard's dad was also thirty-four. Most of the time he was around the house, smoking, playing darts. The only thing he could do well was talk. That was the gift God gave him: he could open strangers to God. Now he was a stranger to the Kingdom, but he had been a Witness since he was six. The whole family on his dad's side were Witnesses. And although Oupa had been a drinker, Gerhard's dad stayed clean. It was only on his thirty-third birthday that Temptation had triumphed; the drink in his blood finally rose up and drowned him.

"Get out with your fucking things!"

In those years Gerhard's dad had found the strength to beat her black and blue, blue and black.

"Stop looking at those bladdy men, dammit! Stop soeking!"

They had been married in Boksburg, half a block from her parents' house, a small, scrubbed church. Methodists. Kafferboeties. The colour wedding photograph stood on the mantelpiece next to a newspaper cutting of the Rugby World Cup team. There was Francois holding the cup above his head. And there was Ma with her mielie sack tits all pregnant with Gerhard. Her tits squeezed out of the white dress that was borrowed from Mrs Noriega who lived next door and whose four daughters and five cousins got married in that same dress with the stain under the armpits.

Gerhard shouted again, "Ma, ice cream! I want an ice cream!" He thought of sitting down, staying on the spot until she turned round and came back to find him. The only problem was that she wouldn't notice - she was too busy wheeling the pram with baby Jacobus into the packed Saturday morning shopping crowds.

Gerhard's dad had kicked his ma until one of her eardrums had burst. They had been sitting on a sofa in her parents' house waiting for George, her younger brother, who ran a garage in Alberton. He had a job for Gerhard's dad as a petrol attendant. It was darkie work but it was worth a few bucks. But Gerhard's dad wasn't happy working for just a few bucks. And when he turned it down, he didn't like it when anyone, least of all Gerhard's ma, called him a 'lazy bastard'.

Gerhard's dad had moved out of Oupa's house when he was seventeen. He had moved into a Station and done Work. Every night he had fought with Satan but he got the better of Satan by comforting the other boys. This way he didn't commit the Sin. The boys also kept him away from the girls who came to the Station wearing white blouses.

When he was twenty-one, Gerhard's dad went down to Durbs to prepare himself for Ordination. He had waited for the Word but no Revelation came. He had prayed and fasted but there was no Revelation. After forty days he had decided that if he could not be a minister, it was better to kill himself. That same day on the beach God sent him Ma.

Ma had long yellow hair. She was a big girl who liked to play games. Gerhard's dad was only too happy to play games.

He couldn't believe his eyes.

The ice cream cart. It was now on their side of the street, on the pavement just ahead of them. The ice-cream seller was shouting out, "Cold . . . cold . . . cold . . . cold! Get one, get one . . . before they're sold!"

"Ma! I want an ice cream!"

She walked on like a duck. But before he could say the word 'ice cream' again, someone knocked against him and the yellow ball in his hand bounced away and rolled into the gutter – and rolled and rolled and rolled, finally being stopped by a cardboard takeaway chicken box.

Gerhard bent down to pick it up, but as he did so, a boy in ragged short pants snatched the ball and darted back into the crowd.

"Hey, stop! Stop!"

At last, Ma turned round. "What's with you, Gerrie? Jesus, this the last time I take you shopping!"

"My ball!"

"Where's your ball?"

"He took my ball!"

"Have you lost it? Who could have taken your ball? What's this nonsense! Gerrie, tell the truth, you've lost it!"

"He grabbed it, ma!"

"Who could have taken your ball in the middle of the pavement?"

"This kaffir boy knocked it out of my hand!"

"That's the last ball I ever buy you, you understand?"

Gerhard looked at her. She would never believe him. She would never buy him an ice cream.

Ma was now standing on the spot where the ball had bounced. And while she was shouting at him, he had looked at her green dress streaked with white marks where their grey cat had scratched. Then he had looked at the three black men in overalls and sneakers with balaclavas pulled over their heads jumping out of a van parked behind her.

The man in front knocked Gerhard down and opened fire on the security guard who was standing with a cocked rifle at the entrance to the First National Bank branch whose steel front door was immediately behind the ice cream-cart. Gerhard watched as the cart blasted open and the suckers in all their rainbow colours scattered across the pavement.

And there, in the middle of the suckers, gasping for breath, his body all mangled and bloody, was the black boy who had picked up the yellow ball that was now bouncing but Gerhard couldn't grab it. The ball bounced once, then twice, then floated up higher and higher, drifting over the buildings to join a peppermint stick and one of the AK47 bullets that had ricocheted off the granite face of the building while the balaclaved men shot their way into the bank and the ice-cream cart oozed out its stickiness.

There was a little lake of ice cream round the blasted bodies of Ma and Baby Jacobus. Gerhard was crying. No, man! The ice cream was not so important and he hadn't meant to hope she should die.

SHE WAS TAKEN CAPTIVE

Kidnappers – a gang of Italians - seize Stella in the street, intending to transport her, send her as a slave-child to another country. But when they surround her, she persuades them to come to her home: she has special things to share with them, valuable treasures. Then, on the way to her house, the Italian men turn into young girls with hard faces who tell her how they will divide up her things.

Stella is unsure whether this switch is to her advantage. Her first thought is that it will be easier to outwit the young girls (the Italians were rough men who stank of wine), but their precociously mean expressions frighten her as much. In fact, the girls jostle and crowd her and push at her breasts. Stella is close to panicking. Do they also intend to sell her? She must outwit them! So she thinks of a new plan, a cheaper and perhaps more effective way to distract them from her prized collection; a plan that may even secure her escape. She persuades the young girls to allow her ten minutes at the neighbourhood shop - and promises to bring back whatever they like: chips, drinks, sweets, chocolate . . .

The girls now embrace her, are so excited that they forget about her other treasures. They give her orders. Stella is jubilant. But she is still fearful. There are so many things on the list, so many things to buy. Her money will be all used up! All the same, what can she do?

She runs to the shop burning with anger and resentment. Is there no way of avoiding this heavy price for her freedom? Then, on the way, she sees her mother's lover drive by in a car. What luck! She waves and calls out. He pulls over. She explains what has happened. He nods his head, but says he is busy - he has to fetch something for her mother. Stella is shocked - there is so little time! Surely he sees the danger? Surely he sees how desperate she is? But he doggedly explains that he must first do what he has to do. Stella begins crying. He relents a little, promises to come back later and help her once he has finished. He drives off.

Stella is heart-broken. And without thinking, cries out, "Stop!"

Her heart jumps. She can hardly believe it! She smiles through her tears. Yes! He is reversing back. He has not let her down.

He throws the car door wide open and runs to her. Again she implores him to lend her money so that she can buy all the sweets the girls want, and still have money left over for herself. He feels her soft hand on his hand, her anguish. She embraces him, promises to save him some sweets.

He gives her money.

She kisses him and runs off to the shop. Everything will turn out well, everything will return to normal. How fortunate her mother's lover also loves sweets!

MYSTERY IN THE COTTAGE

A group of young men make up a soccer team. From time to time they tour villages in their province. On one such occasion they are offered accommodation by a local businessman which they gratefully accept as their financial means are limited and most of their money goes on transport.

The match against the village team is hard fought, but after falling behind, the visitors snatch victory. They are delighted having lost to this team the previous year. Going back to the businessman's house in the late afternoon, they are in the mood to celebrate, and to their delight he offers them several crates of beer as well as a sheep. The young men thank him profusely - such generosity is unusual, especially as his team was on the losing side - but the businessman explains that graciousness in defeat is as important as winning and that by showing them this in practical way he hopes they will take this principle to heart. The young men applaud and prepare to start the feast. The businessman helps make the fire, but as sunset streaks the sky and the braai coals are at their most intense, mutton fat sizzling on the grid, beer wetting their thirsty lips, he receives a telephone call.

His expression darkens - the news is not good. Calling the captain aside, he explains that he must leave immediately, a family emergency has come up and his brother needs help. The captain offers his sympathy, assures him that the team will forgive his departure. Then the businessman leads him to a secluded part of the property, and points to a small cottage. He tells the captain that while he is away, under no circumstance must anyone enter the cottage, it is expressly forbidden to even look inside. The captain is surprised; the cottage seems deserted and quite run down - an unlikely venue for a mystery. But the businessman speaks so vehemently that he holds his tongue and promises that he will relay this message to all the young men and ensure that they obey his ruling.

A few minutes later the businessman leaves and the captain calls the young men together. He informs them in grave tones that no one is to approach the cottage, the prohibition must be absolutely respected; after all, their benefactor may give them additional support if he sees they are responsible. The young men unanimously agree; it will be foolhardy to go against this instruction and they disperse to continue their merrymaking. Indeed, the party mood soars when a group of village women arrive. It seems the fruits of victory are unlimited: who can question their good fortune!

The drinking continues through the night and the businessman does not return. The captain thinks of phoning him to find out if all is well, but decides to respect the man's privacy, and after the umpteenth beer forgets all about him. And he is not alone in this - the whole team is now quite drunk and those who have not managed to pair off with one of the women, lie around on the lawn behind the house, tunelessly singing the latest hit songs. Strangely enough, the match-winning striker is one of these unlucky ones, and at this stage, becoming bored with his companions, decides to explore the furthest reach of the yard. So he staggers away from the womanless group and in his drunken wandering comes across the cottage.

There is a dim light above the front door but the building seems forlorn and abandoned. He is surprised, remembering the captain's urgent recounting of the businessman's warning, and laughs aloud. Why is this old cottage so valuable? Or rather, what is inside that is so valuable? Throwing caution to the wind, he knocks on the door, and to his surprise a quiet voice answers. The voice, that of a woman, asks him to open the door. The striker turns round guiltily - has anyone seen him? He holds back, but the voice is so seductive, so insistent . . . The striker swears, ridiculing his scruples. Surely at this hour, with everyone else either in bed with a local maiden or paralytic on the lawn, he will not be noticed, no harm will be done?

Again the soft voice calls. "Please, please come in! I can't wait to share myself with you. Come, my hero! I have been waiting for so long, so, so long . . ."

The striker blushes. The voice caresses him. His head spins in confusion. In his imagination he sees a lovely, supple woman dressed in a flowing gown; elegant slits down the sides show her well formed legs. He breathes heavily. Of course, she is naked underneath . . .

He turns the doorknob and enters. The house is in darkness.

"Come this way, my beauty," the voice directs him. "Come with me to my bed, come to the love bed . . ."

He hesitates at the threshold, then staggers forward, the voice dancing before him, first on this side, then on that. Entranced, he stumbles deeper into the cottage.

"Come faster, get moving!"

The striker is suddenly overcome with fear. The voice, previously so soft and smooth, is now harsh and commanding. He stops.

"Keep moving you piece of devil!"

Panic-stricken, he turns to leave, but as he does so, hears the door click shut.

"This way, Satan, come to mama, keep walking, come and kiss mama . . ." the voice will not let up; it is now a shriek, a wail.

The young man blunders back to the door. But when he turns the handle, finds it locked. He kicks the door.

"Let me out! Let me out!"

"Walk forward, my lovely! Walk!" There is silence, then "Now I've got you!"

The striker screams as a hand grabs him between his legs and squeezes, a hand that is unnaturally strong for a young woman.

"Leave me! Let go!"

But the hand will not release him and he cannot free himself.

"Want to leave me, my lovely? Still want to leave mama?"

The striker kicks out wildly and to his relief his foot collides with a soft body. There is a savage cry, "Now, now, you ungrateful bastard - now I'll teach you a lesson!" and who ever it is who has enticed him to enter the cottage, grabs the striker's hand and twists it so fiercely that he hears the wrist bone crack. Flooded with pain, the striker collapses and in moments the invisible figure turns him over and beats him viciously with a stick.

*

In the morning they find him on the grass outside the cottage, battered and bloody, but still alive.

Soon after they have taken him to hospital, the businessman returns from his brother. He expresses his anger but it is diluted with remorse.

"I should have known. I should have locked the door."

The captain and the other players stare at him mystified. Why had the door been left open if someone so dangerous had been inside?

"I should have known that a drunken party would lead to trouble. I mean boys will be boys."

"Sir, who was inside?' asks the captain.

"My daughter. She's . . . unwell. We keep her there because the hospital drugs turn her into a zombie and I can't stand to see that. The door's locked from the inside but I've fitted a special device that enables you to open it on the outside. I take her food three times a day and it's easier that way."

The team stands around. The striker has been lucky to survive. They will be back for yet another match in the coming year. Will the businessman still offer them his house? Will they be wise to accept? So much for victory feasts in enemy territory, so much for wandering in the dark!

Meanwhile the striker in hospital is delirious. The voice entreating him to open the door begs him onward, begs him onward . . .

THE FEAST

I am in a darkened hall. At the one end is a row of tables laden with sumptuous foods. A great crowd pushes forward, trying to reach the tables. I, too, am driven by hunger, but hemmed in by a mass of strangers, pressed against the entrance door, I am stuck at the very back.

Scents and bouquets of rare flowers, wines and incense fill the air, mingling with the rich aromas rising from the tables. All eyes are directed towards the polished tureens filled with steaming soups and stews, the earthen-ware dishes laden with tender, well-spiced meats, fishes and vegetables, the porcelain bowls brimming with sauces, salads and succulent desserts. And peering through the half-light, I anxiously watch the silhouettes of those at the front, their heads moving this way and that as they heap their plates and eat their fill. I watch their every movement, their every gulp, till these fortunate ones (oh, so reluctantly!) at last concede their privileged places and make way for others.

The hours pass. Little by little, the groaning, famished crowd advances, each row of the needy finally reaching the tables, able to feast, till I, too, weak and tense, reach the front. But to my distress, I cannot find a plate - the neat stacks that had earlier stood on the tables have all been used. I search under baskets of fruit but the plates hidden there are crusted with dried out leftovers.

I search under bowls and jugs; the few I find are also dirty and chipped. I search under the tables but only find crumbs and broken vessels. Meanwhile the hall fills with the sounds of grunting satisfaction. If I do not find a clean plate soon, the food will be finished! I tilt the heaviest pot but all I find is a heap of tangled, sticky cutlery.

And though I redouble my efforts, shifting and lifting, checking everywhere, my search is fruitless. What more can I do? It would be unseemly to eat with my fingers. And so, frantic as I am, frustrated by my failure and unnerved by the hisses of those behind me – they are becoming viciously impatient at my wasting time - I turn away from the tables and drift back to the exit. There is nothing to be done; I must contain my hunger.

I leave the hall and return to the small room where I live. Still distraught, my empty stomach rumbling with disappointment and anger, I lie down to rest. But images of the feast float before my eyes, each succulent dish mockingly parading before me, an endless procession of mouth-watering delicacies. And I curl up, choked by an anguished appetite, and eventually, after many hours, fall asleep.

At daylight I rise and return to the hall. The containers and receptacles have all been replenished, enormous piles of clean plates and heaps of clean cutlery are attractively laid out. Again the perfume of incense and the aromas of food fill the air, and masses of people push forward. But this time I am almost immediately near the front of the crowd and within minutes I excitedly stand before the freshly decorated, laden tables.

At last, I have achieved my aim; I can pile up a plate and satisfy my hunger. But I do not move. The feast is spread out before me in all its richness, but I stand quietly composed. I am content to wait. I am content to contemplate.

THE CAMP

Abel is in a concentration camp. It is made up of old wooden houses that line a vast network of canals filled with cold, stagnant water. It is not clear if the camp has been evacuated, or if most of the imprisoned have already died of starvation or been murdered for there seem to be very few people, a handful of prisoners in each building, and there are no obvious signs of guards or soldiers. Abel sleeps on the first floor of one of the broken down buildings. Several inmates sleep in rooms on one side of the ground floor. On the other side is a large, open space shaped like a ballroom.

It is early morning. There is a sense of inertia; time does not seem to move. The people living on the ground floor slowly wake. They rise to their feet, and one behind the other, create a human chain. Shuffling dejectedly, they enter the ballroom, treading on the smashed remnants of everyday things - pots, plates, books, tools - scattered across the floor, the debris of ordinary life. And Abel, hearing the relentless dragging of feet, leaves his sleeping place and joins them - joins the listless file, moving this way and that as they endlessly circle the ballroom.

He walks automatically, barely aware of his surroundings. Then he realizes that as well as trampling on the things they know so intimately, have in the past sometimes treasured but often used with indifference, they are also stepping on mounds of human faeces; and that faeces is smeared all over the ballroom - on the floor, on the pillars that support the ceiling, on the walls. However, the other prisoners show no concern. Abel tries to attract their attention, shakes them. How can they be so oblivious to the stench and the ugliness? They must act! Such a life is intolerable! But he is ignored. And to his amazement, more and more prisoners from outside the house drift in and join the line.

Hours pass. He persists, entreats person after person. Still no one seems to share his anger. And gradually his will to rebel subsides and he, too, retreats into a sullen blankness. The procession moves robotically, without talking, without touching, one behind the other, snaking round the ground floor impervious to their degradation. The chain becomes longer and longer. The hall is soon crowded. Then a thought crosses his mind, one that is distasteful to him and yet which pushes other thoughts away: he must hurry to safeguard his sleeping place on the first floor, protect it from the swelling number of new people. By evening, completely drained by the mind-numbing, compulsive parade, they will not be able to leave this building, and desperately needing rest, will fall asleep wherever they can squeeze their bodies.

Darkness falls. The ground floor is densely packed. Abel watches with alarm as a mass of inmates spill towards the stairway that leads to the first floor. He does not wish to hurt anyone, but he will have to be resolute, act quickly to protect what is his. He pushes his way through the crowd, walks up. But when he reaches his sleeping place it is already taken. There is a woman lying there with a child. He looks down at the little girl. Her eyes are closed. How innocent she seems! The floor is covered with the bodies of broken people, crushed together, seeking warmth. Yes, they have been defeated. But the child must be allowed to dream.

Slowly, painfully, Abel tries to make enough space to lie down at her feet.

*

The following night he is still in his rags in the ballroom. A crowd of people stream in. Standing alone in a balcony fitted to one side, he watches them fill the space. But the ballroom is now an auditorium and the people are in good health, warmly dressed in autumn clothes; fit, comfortable, lively, they wait patiently for the start of a performance, the presentation of a work of art.

Abel observes the gathering with fervent interest. And though his eyes and cheeks are dark from hunger and disease, perhaps terminally weakened, he feels at rest, fascinated by these contented, if un-exceptional people seated in the spotlessly clean, simply decorated yet pleasing auditorium that slants with rows of seats.

The performance begins. He scans their faces. And he draws strength from their stimulation and enjoyment. Indeed, as the audience becomes more and more focused, engrossed by the perform-ance, Abel is ever more appreciative of their absorption, their atten-tiveness to each nuance and shift. What joy to be able to witness and share their love of beauty! He feels calm, studying the faces of these easeful but serious people seated in the concentration camp, an audi-ence that breathes with well-being and vitality.

*

The day after this performance Abel is out walking. The canals glint with sunlight, the air is fresh. Though still dressed in rags, he does not appear deprived or ravaged. On the contrary - he feels buoy-ant and relaxed, walking energetically towards an ancient building whose basic design is traditional, quite simple, but which has been elaborately renovated. It could be an art gallery or some other kind of cultural centre.

Abel is attracted by the building and excited to be reaching it, but the closer he gets to the imposing columns and monumental entrance, the more disquiet he feels: something is not right - it is too new and too neat, too spruced up. And yet he maintains his brisk pace, for despite his growing concern at the artificial renovation of the build-ing, it is a truly uplifting day. Then, to add to his positive spirit, he recognizes a woman standing beside one of the columns. She was one of the prisoners in the old brown house, one of those who had walked so passively with him in the human chain. But on this bright, sun-strewn morning, she is dressed in a vivid red suit, her face has fleshed out, she glows with confidence, radiates pride. And she offers him a warm greeting, only to suddenly draw back.

Agitatedly, almost disbelieving, she asks why he still lives in the camp, why he continues to wear rags.

Abel answers, "Like you, I want to live. And I do not want my anger to replace or destroy beauty. But I am dismayed by the shiny reconstruction of this building - the bricks have replaced the living wood. I do not need the artificial to uplift me. And though I am not perfumed, I am clean. As you see me, I am whole again - like the audience at the performance who filled the ballroom with their profound enjoyment."

She does not reply, standing against the towering, freshly plastered and painted columns. And he knows that she does not believe him, but he does not begrudge her a new life. He stands at peace beside her in his rags.

SHE IS ALONE

S he is lying down. The bed stands in an otherwise empty room - there is only a stool and a very small table on which she has placed a kettle, two cups, a pot, a plate and some cutlery. A suitcase with her clothes lies open in a corner. She shares the flat with two other families but is fortunate enough to have a small room to herself. In any case they start work early in the morning and drop their children at a crèche so for most of the day she is the only one in the flat.

She knows some people in this new country; they are distant relatives from where she grew up. But she feels very isolated and alone this morning, and lies, legs sprawled, as if she is drunk, but she is not drunk just sweating, for the city is hot, not as hot and humid as her old city, but still steamy with sun and rain.

At first it was exciting, this very big city compared to her home, this city with a famous name: a place where they said money can be made, where new things can be learned, where you can change your life. And there are many hundreds of thousands from all over the continent who have come here. They fill this suburb; everywhere in the streets one sees their robes and hears their languages, and sees their shop signs.

She has been here six months. Her relatives tried to help, but they could not find her work. It was only two weeks ago that she found a job in a small shop selling vegetables. The owner, though not from her hometown, was from the same region and speaks the same dialect. He pays her almost nothing, but he is polite, and in the evenings after he checks the day's takings and locks up, he gives her a lift back to the flat.

Sprawled on the bed, she is curled into herself. A magazine lies on the floor. Her face is grey with fatigue. She does not know if it is worth anything to still have hope. She turns over. She wants to cry but she knows that crying will not help. She has cried too many times already this morning. Why has he fired her? It was not true that she had taken money from the till. It was not her fault that the shop was not making a profit.

*

Dawn light does not wake her. She had been to a club. She had only taken soft drinks. No beer could tempt her. She saw what happened to women who touched beer. Men had danced with her. Her dance was a flurry of limbs, of jiving hips that sucked them in, made them gasp and grab at her. But she had not allowed them to touch - not even her waist or her hands. And when one of them had offered her money, she had shouted 'no' and pushed him away. Other women had watched her jealously. But the man she had hoped to see had not arrived. This was the second time he had not turned up. Was he with one of her friends? Another woman from the old town?

When the moon was already dipping, she'd walked back to the flat. A drunk man crossed the road. She'd walked faster. And when he had come up to her, and lunged at her breasts, she had taken off her shoes and run away. Now she sleeps. And when she wakes it is long past noon.

What is happening to her in this new country? Is life here better than at home doing the housework for her parents? She turns over. Maybe she should have gone off with one of the men, the one with the black jacket, the smooth head.

I am under your spell O African woman whom I love.

This note lies in her bag; it had been given to her by a grey haired man. He had lingered at her table. Then he had sat down and taken her hand, taken her attention from other suitors. The old man had become an embarrassment. But when he had offered to take her to dinner, she had agreed. And after dinner, when he had dropped her back at the flat, she had sat stubbornly in the car, refused to hold his hand, waiting for 'airtime' money. The next time she had kissed him and he had given her 'grocery' money. But the following night when he had wanted to caress her, she had run out. And afterwards, though he had begged her to accept him 'flesh to flesh', he was not violent so she had continued to see him and only scolded him if his payments became smaller.

The real problem was the drug. The drug had been given to her by the brother of one her school-friends. He had said it was good for the stomach and made you relax. And yes, the little white pill had made her feel loose, so loose that she had slept with him and two other men that night. The hot beat of his sound system had made her forget all her problems. There was no doubt: despite the jagged edges of the next morning, the headache and the dry tongue, it had been good, the drug - very good. And she was ready for him the next night. And the next.

But later that week, without understanding why, when they had gone to a flat in an area she did not know well, she had refused to sleep with more than one man, and the bringer of the drug was angry. "I invite my friends because I want them to also enjoy. Who are you to refuse?" His friends had tried to restrain him but he had beaten her, and she had cried - from the blows and because she had not wanted to believe he was so stupid, this man she quite liked.

It is three months since that night. She is sad. His rejection is petty. She still desires him. The drug makes her feel she can go on till dawn because her body is supercharged liquid, ebbing and flowing with the tides of her skin and blood. But though she had bought it from someone else afterwards, and it was as good as before, it is expensive and she cannot afford it.

Now she lies on her bed, sweating, head throbbing. The only compensation is that the older man will be arriving soon. How long will it take till he comes?

*

The church was not far from the flat. She remembered always seeing it but not stopping to really look at it; this church that was an old house with a big sign that read CHURCH OF LOVE. She had laughed at the name. Laughed aloud because it was such a good idea: that a church be devoted to love. It had made her think bitterly of the man who had first pushed her down and broken her maidenhood. He was a preacher who had a flock of goats and two houses but his teeth were rotten and his dead wife had been a witch. Only her sister has guessed at her secret: she does not want to go back home because she would be forced to marry that man. Another computer course, that was what she needed - not a husband. The work she wanted to do, in an office making more money her family had ever dreamed of, demanded such knowledge.

Her father had borrowed from relatives and a loan shark to send her to this city. Now she is on her bed in the room she shares with her sister; her older sister who has just arrived in this city and already knows what to do. (Her sister is at work; she is always on time for work and is studying at night for a higher diploma.) Yes, she lies on her bed crying because she has failed her computer test and is scared of what her father will say. And her sister has already told her she must go back home and marry the preacher. No, she wants to stay in this city. She is sure she will find work soon. She wants to stay and learn new things that will make her life more rewarding. She wants certain things that home cannot give her.

She sits up on her bed. She has made up her mind: she will rewrite the test; she will pass. She will find a man here. They will walk down the aisle of the CHURCH OF LOVE. She will only go back home when all this has come true. She opens the curtains and the sun streams in.

She shivers with knowledge. This city will give her what she needs. But the choices that need to be made are hers alone. Hers alone. She knows this as the doorbell rings.

BLUE

Why do certain images, rather than others, lodge in the mind, resurfacing long after they have imprinted themselves; whether in dreams, snatches of hallucination or reverie, or as fragments of music bursting from the air while trapped in traffic jams, while cooking, washing or making love.
The film is entitled 'Blue': depressed, lonely, melancholy.
But blue is also: peace, freedom, space, tranquility.

S hirley found the film unconvincing. Why was the main character, Julie, so unrevealing of her feelings? It was to be expected that at first she would be numbed by grief - her husband, Patrice, a famous composer, and their young daughter, had been killed in a car accident - but surely there would be a point when she would react openly and express her anguish and her rage, her sense of impotence? In addition, there was the obvious danger that if she bottled up her grief, any one of these emotions could spiral out of control and result in breakdown. However, at the other extreme, if she was wise, there was the possibility of transcendence, in the form of gentleness, leading to an empathy with all people and an understanding of shared pain, a humility built on feeling all losses. Surely the mask would drop? The emotional disfigurement and the vacuum would be unveiled, she would begin to exorcize her grief, start out again on the torturous road and reconcile with living.

*

Julie finds herself watching television. The program is about Patrice. Oliver, Patrice's long-standing assistant, displays a photograph. It is of Patrice and another woman, his mistress. During all the years of

their marriage, Julie has had no suspicion of her husband's involve-
ment in another relationship. The revelation is shattering. She is both
dulled and enraged. Was her past happiness real if at the same time
he was simultaneously so close to another woman?

*

Juliet Binoche, the actress who plays the part of Julie, is slightly built,
yet conveys a sense of great inner power and control. Shirley greatly
admires her poise, her quality of grace softened by woundedness. At
times she is so absorbed by Binoche that the dialogue flows past her,
becoming a stream of sound that dissolves into all other auditory
components: cars, telephones, the music of orchestras rising . . .

*

Mourning, a woman is thrown into overpowering isolation. While
she lives suspended, not knowing if her suffering will end, she hears,
in her subconscious, fragments of the music her husband had been
composing, his unfinished "Hymn to Unity", to love and solidarity, to
a new age of peace and creativity in a United Europe. But this music
is not his composition alone: the key elements have been created by
his wife. And with his death, it is finally given to her to complete.

*

Blue: crystals, a lollipop, a rubbish bag, jeans, a mattress, a pen for
correcting music scores. Above all, a pool of blue water in which
Julie immerses herself; into which sorrow and tension are released
and transformed.

*

Juliette Binoche has short, dark hair that clings round her pale, white
face like a helmet. She seems boyish, yet is sensual in a feminine
way. Shirley watches her move. There is a coolness that occasion-
ally falters but never visibly alters. The mask remains intact. There is
only silence and sadness. Where has she locked up the scream that
is surely festering in her, trying to force a way out but being pushed
back to writhe in her guts?

Despite Shirley's immediate reaction, that the film isn't entirely
credible, that there are sections bordering on melodrama, it has dis-

turbed her, this story of a bereaved woman who discovers that her husband was secretly involved with another woman and that it is this woman who is to bear his child into the future.

Holding a carton of popcorn in one hand and a large paper cup of cold drink in the other, Shirley watches Julie scrape her fingers against a stonewall till they bleed.

*

In the dark cell of the movie house, a man in a denim jacket shuffles up the stairs. He enters a row of seats, brushes against Shirley's legs and sits down.

The present is always a precipice.

*

Julie sleeps with Oliver on the night after the accident. Why does this happen?

On his side the motivation is clear: he has always loved her - but from a distance. Secondly, he wants her help in finishing the "Hymn to Unity". On her side the motivation is more complicated. Is it that she seeks momentary comfort for her pain? Or is it that she feels a violent need to uproot the past?

She leaves him in the morning.

*

Julie swims, slowly tires and exhilarates the body. Fragments of melody visit her, threads of the hymn.

The text of the "Hymn to Unity" is taken from an ancient Greek poem:

"Without love, one has nothing,
Though one flies with angels' wings.
Without love, one is heavy as a base metal."

*

The young man slouches, massages his crotch. Shirley ignores him. He continues to play with himself, insisting on her attention. She does not know what to do. The film is very absorbing but he is becoming aggressively exhibitionistic.

"Go away, you stupid man," she calls out. "I'm going to call the manager."

The man stops playing with himself.

*

It is difficult to believe that Julie can contain her pain without breaking down. It is more difficult to believe that she accepts and befriends her husband's mistress; and instead of being overwhelmed by bitterness and fury, congratulates her on being pregnant, and offers her the beautiful old house where she and Patrice had shared so much.

It is difficult to believe in such generosity of spirit.

*

At the end of the film, Shirley and the man both remain seated. The audience files out. The cleaners dawdle in. Shirley refuses to make the first move. She wants the young man to go out, wants him to be gone so that she can again visualize and experience the cinema as it was before his arrival and assault on her senses. She wants to purify the atmosphere of his coarseness, his obsession.

She tells one of the cleaners what has happened. The woman laughs. The man is well known at the complex. He has been thrown out several times. She is surprised that he has managed to sneak back in.

The young man jumps over the seat in front of him and runs out.

*

Shirley stands up. It is late afternoon. What is she to do?

She strolls out into the mall, stops in front of various shop windows and looks at displays of clothes, jewelry, furniture, gardening equipment and medicines. Then she looks at the crowds of people in restaurants and fast food stores - well-groomed men and women talking to each other, shopping bags propped against their chairs.

The hymn is singing itself and she feels hungry.

ALL AGAINST ALL

A bel is depressed, weighed upon by a multitude of pressures. He decides to leave the city and seek relief. In this spirit he drives out, and reaching the outskirts, comes upon a forest.

The forest, which has been planted by a pulp company, is made up of commercial pine trees. They stretch in neat rows for a vast distance. Indeed, it is so vast that the naked eye cannot see to its limits. And Abel is both attracted and perplexed: the vastness is pleasing, but the conformity of the rows disappoints; and to make matters worse, a high fence cuts it off from the city. So, though he pulls off the highway and parks next to the fence, and sits surveying the green mass, he is undecided. On the one hand, it is very tempting to stay, and find a way (force a way?) into the forest - despite the sameness it will surely be relaxing to walk leisurely down the endless rows. On the other hand, should he not push on and try to find a more stimulating, more varied environment? Irritated, he slouches morosely in his car. But then, after some time, he notices a small gate in the fence and the gate decides him.

Abel locks the car and enters the forest. After walking for just a few minutes he is pleased to find a path. And the path quickly takes him deep into the forest, the disciplined rows of pine giving way on either side to a thick tangle of natural growth. Indeed, how misleading outer appearances can be! Almost as soon as the fringe was penetrated, the forest became a mass of indigenous foliage, in fact, a jungle. Yet, to his astonishment, the path not only remains defined and easy to follow, but is carpeted with a thick layer of leaves that cushions his feet and promotes a springy rhythm.

He strolls deeper and deeper into this jungle. The air is fresh and sweet; colourful plants and flowers grow in profusion; the bird life is diverse and musical. And he is thrilled to have found (so close to the city) such a tranquil and edifying environment. Then, to add to his pleasure, a group of young boys appear. They walk sprightly along, offer friendly greetings as they pass. Truly the forest is a benign environment!

The day passes slowly. The path meanders on, new delights appearing round every turn. But as evening approaches, Abel realizes that he has walked for several hours (almost in a trance), and that now, as darkness sets in, the car is far behind, and he has no food or water or cover for the night. He stops. Should he turn round and walk back to the gate? Or should he calmly make a bed with the masses of pine needles? He stands, uncertain. But before he can come to a decision, he is shaken by a loud roar - a savage and very menacing roar. The roar is repeated; clearly the night creatures, asleep in the thick foliage during the day, are now growing active. Soon there is a cacophony of howling. How wrong he was about the nature of the forest! These predators will certainly threaten his life! There is no option - he must walk back to the gate though the gathering gloom makes seeing difficult and the roars grow nearer.

Abel sets off. He moves fast despite his hunger pangs. Indeed, he feels well, for despite this unexpected danger the day has been remarkably fulfilling. Then suddenly he hears a rustling. He turns - two enormous, glowing eyes glare up at him. He freezes. What is he to do? To run will not prevent the beast (is it a leopard?) from pouncing on him. No, there is only one solution. Quietly and very slowly he steps backwards. The eyes are huge. They do not blink, staring up at him, reflecting back the rising moonlight. Slowly, very slowly, he inches carefully away from the beast that lies in the bushes.

The night is very still. The eyes remain fixed on him, but he progresses steadily backwards, retreating deeper into the jungle. Relentlessly, they follow his passage, and he knows he must keep on, even if movement simply postpones the inevitable attack. The minutes pass, the eyes follow but miraculously keep their distance. Abel breathes easier. Then without warning, he trips and his ankle gives way. Grunting with pain on the forest floor, he is completely helpless. Trying to move further is impossible. So he lies, sprawled on the path. But after his initial shock, he feels strangely calm. And the yellow eyes glow but are somehow less terrifying.

He stretches his throbbing legs, feels drowsy; soon he cannot keep his eyes open. And later that night, while he dreams that the city has disappeared and the forest has been abandoned by the pulp company - there is no pretence that it is owned, managed, utilized for gain - the beast slides out of the bushes, and licks his eyelids.

*

In the morning Abel rises, and feeling greatly refreshed, makes his way back to the gate. On the way he passes the same group of boys who were hiking. He greets them. They show no sign of remembering him but respond politely. And when he finds that the gate is gone and the fence no longer encircles the forest, he has a sense of a new world opening up, and he feels enthusiasm for it - there is work to do, and he will be equal to the task.

EXCURSION

I am with a group of workers; we visit a sanctuary for pelicans. We watch massed flocks rise, and fly, and land.

At lunchtime, the guide, a young Coloured man, leads us to shady area where we sit down to eat. While we are eating, he remarks that if every White family's wealth was appropriated by a Black family, the Black family would be able to live off that store of resources without ever having to work again; indeed, the Black family would have more than enough for the whole of their lives.

The workers murmur agreement. The man next to me looks at my bare arms, sun-burnt but pale against his skin. He says he will take what I have. I feel angry, but decide there is no point in saying anything - it is not that the crowd is threatening, they know me, I have been long in 'The Struggle', I am not like all the other Whites; everyone knows that.

The workers leave. I am left to clean up the mess of papers and fruit peels from lunch. The guide reappears and observes that I am doing a good job throwing all the rubbish down a storm drain.

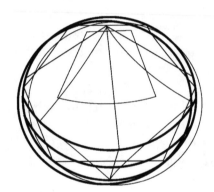

ESCALATOR

A man visits a holiday resort. He wanders from the funfair to the promenade, from the beach to the strip of restaurants.

In the playground he meets a woman with short dark hair and a plain face. Below her shoulder blade is a tattoo - a tiny mermaid. While her son runs from the swings to the merry-go-round, from the seesaw to the slide, they fall into conversation. There is an easy familiarity about their contact. She expresses the hope that he also has a young son, that the two can play together, but he smiles apologetically - he is childless.

They leave the playground and join a throng of holidaymakers who are entering the resort's greatest attraction - a gigantic, self-contained 'Planet of Marvels'. The entry point is via an escalator that leads up into the bowels of an enormous airborne bubble. As they ascend with the elevator into the bubble, they have an unbroken view of the endless blue ocean. And once they enter the dome, they join a queue at the entrance to the first Marvel.

This first Marvel is an anthill with human proportions; they walk about in the endless tunnels scented with the most varied perfumes of fresh earth. The second is a beehive; undressed, they are coated and lick the honey spilling from the wax. The third is a spider web that runs up and down just above the surface of the ocean and sways with the breeze; they climb the strands and swing gaily across the water. The fourth is a human womb; they loll about in the evanescent warmth, the rich fluid sustaining, nourishing them till they feel reborn.

So they spend the day moving from one Marvel to another, experiencing and rejoicing at these human simulations of nature's bounty.

And when the sun begins to set, and they are ready to leave the bubble, they feel as if they have always been together. But it is time to part. She must return home. She explains that she is gratified to have met him, but that she is not ready for a new partner. Perhaps they will meet again when she has cast off her sorrow.

They shake hands; she touches him on the face. Then she turns away with the boy, and he is left alone at the foot of the bubble. He looks up at the gigantic, glittering sphere. How extraordinary an achievement! He claps his hands, at once exhilarated, at once regretful. But then he smiles, a wistful, soft smile: whatever the future will bring, this day of fateful bonding will remain buoyant in his memory - indestructible, another true marvel.

OUT OF THE WRECKAGE

I am a soldier in an army. It is night. I sit on a bed in front of a locker. Each soldier has a locker. The locker room is on the ground floor of a large white building that is seven or eight storeys high. I carefully pack my locker with various things.

To the north of the building are avenues and trees and other buildings. Here, in a secluded side street, I have parked a brand-new white car. I place the keys to this car in a magazine of bullets that I hide in the locker. Then I leave the locker room and walk out of the building.

I go to an area of desolate, bare earth that lies on the south side. I am very tired. It is time to sleep, but there is no bed or any other comfortable surface on which to rest. I have no choice. I lie down on the depleted, dusty earth. In the dark I am just able to make out two other men, one of whom I recognize as a colleague from work; the other I cannot place. We acknowledge each other with gestures but do not speak. Then we close our eyes.

I am half asleep when a great rumbling disturbs me. I open my eyes. The white building is vibrating. The entire top floor shakes violently. I am alarmed, but there does not seem to be any immediate danger. I decide to go back to sleep. However, as soon as I close my eyes, huge chunks of masonry begin raining down; pieces of brickwork, window frames and doors - an avalanche which incredibly only falls onto the bare, parched stretch of land to the south and not onto the green, built-up north.

The downpour intensifies, becomes more threatening. I realize that at any moment a piece of falling debris might injure or even kill me. I begin to panic. Then, within me, a voice says, "Do not move.

Stay calm. Wait." The hail of objects continues but, despite my great fear, I manage to contain myself.

Suddenly the white building collapses. With a single, continuous motion - like a wave - it topples over and, landing with a shattering crash, causes a massive, choking cloud of dust to rise into the air. Disbelieving, I stagger to my feet. The storm of masonry is over. I am saved! Then I think about my locker and the new car.

I force my way into the ruins of the building, burrowing through the rubble till I reach the locker room. Digging frantically, tossing bricks and pieces of wood aside, I search everywhere. There it is! My locker is still intact.

I open the locker and remove the magazine of bullets. The keys are where I had stashed them. Then I step out of the building and walk quickly to the north side to find that, still surrounded by trees and greenery, the new, white car is parked where I had left it - gleaming and whole, untouched, ready to drive.

SHE WHOM I LOVE

She aroused within him a sensation he could not adequately describe: no other woman, including his wife, had ever caused him to be so fascinated by her containment, her aura of at-homeness in the world; a generous and candid self-sufficiency that radiated power and worth.

They both work for an insurance company. He is a middle level manager. She is a clerk - together with thirty other clerks, all women - and she reports to him. They have worked together for several months and are well aware that they are both married and have children and take their family responsibilities seriously.

When she had first started working, he had been attracted to her not just because she was new, and hence unknown. Sitting opposite him in his office, when they had discussed her duties and he had detailed his expectations, the modest but sure way in which her eyes had engaged him was enough for him to realize that she was no devious office politician, no flirt, nor ideological feminist challenging him for the sake of it.

Her questions had been thoughtful and well directed and he had answered in his customarily friendly and obliging way. And while these exchanges had taken place, he had carefully, but not obviously, examined her features, her breasts, her waist, her legs . . . all the while absorbing the pleasing cadences of her voice. Then he had escorted her to the floor where her department was stationed. And as they had walked together past the other clerks, he had touched her naked arm with his hand, and let it linger. She had immediately broken contact. But soon afterwards, perhaps because she had withdrawn, but not in a panicky or too abrupt way, when leaving her with the line manager, he had shaken her hand formally and sought to hold it as long as he could. Again she had not allowed prolonged contact, had not allowed her hand to remain clasped with his for more time than was polite; and yet the rebuff had not injured him, nor caused him to be resentful. Her manner had been so gracious, so assured and understanding that he had not taken her withdrawal as a sign of disinterest, but merely as a statement that she was not in a position to respond more openly because of circumstances.

*

They have contact several times a day about different administration issues: sometimes on the phone, sometimes by email; sometimes in his office and sometimes in hers. And their meeting regularly attracts no attention from other staff members as it is well explained by the rhythms and needs of work.

However, in the privacy of his office, over the months, on many occasions, in passing her documents or in receiving them from her, he has tried to touch or hold her. And each time, she has gently, but firmly, withdrawn. And though he has also, though very rarely and with great trepidation, caressed her back and neck (he has done so fleetingly without exposing his desire too grossly), she has reacted with dignity and restraint. Indeed, in the aftermath of these intimacies, she has always smiled: a wry smile acknowledging his attentions as a compliment even if they could not be extended. And so, to his great relief, their relationship remains friendly and unstrained despite these one-sided and dubious liberties. And it is therefore no surprise when the retrenchments proposed by top management are entrusted to him, and the office explodes into factionalism, and he has to select those to be dismissed and negotiate their packages, that she defends him to her sister clerks, pointing out that he is trying to minimize the job losses and maximize the payouts, and that, in any event, the decision has been taken against his advice. Similarly, it is natural that he greatly values this support, relying on her to turn the animosity and suspicion of the staff away from him to those who were in fact responsible. And when he succeeds in halving the job cuts and doubling the compensatory payouts, he is thrilled by her public expression of gratitude at a staff meeting.

He thanks her afterwards in his office. And when she rises to leave, he takes her hand, and this time she does not remove hers. He is overwhelmed with expectation, but when he tries to embrace her, and kisses her neck, she slips away.

*

Routine work resumes. He is now more inflamed than ever, begins to manufacture spurious reasons for calling her to his office. She tries to deflect him with her customary grace and good nature, but his advances grow more and more insistent, crude, so that she makes every effort to avoid being alone with him. Then, as is to be expected, her avoidance causes him to feel ashamed, and quite maddened. Fearful of arousing the suspicion of the other clerks, hoping against hope, he continues to instruct her to come to his office. And when he again tries to be intimate, she begs him to restrain himself. Soon afterwards she withdraws completely, refuses altogether to come to his office, insists that he either telephone or come down to her floor where he has to be controlled because they will be seen by others. His humiliation is acute; he despairs. How is he to rebuild her confidence, her respect? Depression and frustration sour his life. He thinks of resigning, of relocating to another city. But he knows this sense of failure, of incompleteness, will not be so easily banished.

Then, one day without notice, she comes to his office. He is overjoyed but also uneasy. Given the past, he cannot believe she has come to offer herself. She closes the door. He watches her take a seat. To his dismay she is uncharacteristically evasive, unfocussed. And when eventually she gets to the point - she needs compassionate leave, time to prepare for a complex and demanding court action - he grows more alarmed: is she is initiating a charge against him, an action for harassment that will destroy his life? He waits with rising fear. Her expression grows more anguished. Then she begins crying, and despite his wariness, he wishes to comfort her. But suddenly she says that she and her husband are divorcing and he is filled with elation. What a change of circumstance! She would still be a mother with children but she would be available. Available? He turns the word over. How he wants to hold her, caress her, kiss her . . . No, he cannot wait and dream forever. He loves his wife and he loves this woman. Why can he not love them both?

"Compassionate leave to prepare for your divorce?"

"I need time for the trial. My husband wants custody of our children. He says I am not a fit mother because I have been having an affair with you. He says he has proof. He won't listen to me. Just because I told him how much I like and admire you does not mean that we sleep together! So what if I used to stay behind in the evenings to help you with the backlog? Did that mean I don't love him! In any case, he used to come to the office some nights and wait for me to finish. He saw there was nothing between us. Now I have to fight for my kids!"

She cries again, looks away

He leaves his chair, goes to her, touches her arm. "Please . . . I'll do anything to help. Just tell me."

"Help? Of course you can help!"

"Just tell me how." He pauses. "You know how I feel about you."

She nods, seems to smile through her tears. But when he tries to hold her, she stops him.

"You love your wife and children - don't you? Of course you do! You know what it means . . ." She stands up, shaking. "If I lose my children I'll never forgive you! You must give evidence at the trial. You must clear me! You must come and tell the court the truth. We have never been lovers and never will be. Isn't that so?"

He watches her leave the room. He loves this woman. He watches her leave the room and he wonders how it will be to work with her every day and carry this between them.

*

A week before the divorce trial, her lawyer arranges for him to meet her husband. They have a long talk and as a result the husband agrees to reconcile with her. The day after, she comes to his office and thanks him, gives him a hug. He is sad. To think he will never caress her. But just as bitter is the realization that it is probably for the best.

THE SICK MAN

E very night Abel finds a sick man in his bed. And night after night
he administers medicine, provides food and clean bedclothes,
because he feels compassion, wants to aid the sick man, wants to heal
him. But sadly, no matter what medicine or treatment he provides,
nothing helps - the sick man does not recover. Indeed, the sick man
grows weaker and weaker; and as the illness intensifies, so he rebels,
cursing his fate, calling down revenge on those he believes have caused
him such misery, those who have failed to alleviate his suffering.
And this reprobation hurts Abel, although, at the same time, he is
sympathetic, knowing that pain and fear can cause people to lose
perspective. Moreover, to complicate matters further there is a part
of him that fears he is not doing enough, is being lazy, inattentive. So
he endures the abuse, continues to serve the sick man as best he can.

Months pass in this way. Abel sacrifices all his other commitments,
neglects his wife, barely attends to his children. However, nothing
can arrest the dying man's degeneration, and Abel becomes more
and more distressed. And, then, after a series of particularly severe
attacks, the sick man dies. Shocked, Abel mourns his passing. How
sad that he could not be restored to good health! And yet, to his
secret shame, there is also a sense of relief - indeed, a two fold relief.
For that night he dreams of the sick man also celebrating his having
finally found peace. Thus when Abel awakes, he is for the first time
(since the arrival of the sick man in his bed), refreshed, relieved of
frustration and worry.

The next day he goes about his work cheerfully, the world is again
a place of joy and beauty. He laughs with his wife, plays games with
his children. But that night, when he lies down to sleep, he is horri-

fied to find another sick man beside him. And this sick man, too, is entirely dependent on him for his every need.

Abel feels overwhelmed, resentful. Why is he being singled out by these miserable, disease-ridden people? He hates himself for these thoughts, but try as he may to banish them, they rise up, carried high on the smell of the sick man's body. So he curses his fate, considers abandoning the groaning man, but in the end (such is his devotion to the ideal of solidarity), that despite his dismay, he resolves to heal him; and bearing in mind his previous experience, studies the sick man's symptoms with even greater care than before. Then, at the end of a thorough process of diagnosis, he purchases medicine at great cost to himself and his family, and unstintingly provides for all the sick man's many daily needs.

The weeks pass. Redoubling his commitment, Abel continues to devote himself to finding a cure. But, as before, the sick man does not strengthen, the disease wastes him further; and like his predecessor, in seeking reasons for his failure to recover, begins to upbraid him for neglect. Abel is at first appalled. How can his efforts again be so unappreciated? However, being more hardened to unjustified criticism (though a part of him still remains in doubt as to his level of service), he sets aside these comments and carries on with his nursing. In fact, caring for the sick man pushes him to the point of exhaustion. But then, before he reaches a state of terminal burnout, the sick man suffers a fatal stroke, and Abel must organize his burial.

Abel turns the last sod onto the sick man's grave. The nightmare is finally over. At last, he can breathe and return to the life he once lived! A life that now, more than ever, he recognizes to be full and satisfying. He will return home. His wife and children will finally enjoy his unreserved attention. Neighbours will visit, wishing him well.

He rejoins his family. But then, alone in the evening when they have all gone to bed, he is stricken with remorse: they were right, he has not tried hard enough - that is why the sick men have died. He has been negligent, too self-absorbed, uncaring; and this second failure implies that he is congenitally incapable of serving the needy, irredeemably selfish and unworthy. He sits with a book and reads, though he does not digest what he reads, he is too preoccupied with his sense of failure. In fact, he beats himself before eventually falling asleep.

The next morning Abel wakes well satisfied to find yet another sick man beside him, his condition as acute as the others. And he rejoices. Now he will have an opportunity to finally prove himself! He will tend the sick man so expertly, with such diligence and tenderness, that he will surely survive his malady and go on to live a healthy and meaningful life. With this belief, Abel goes about his nursing with a sense of salvation. Day by day he helps and sustains the sick man, again neglecting his family. And yet, despite this special attentions, in a replay of the past, the sick man does not heal and begins to condemn Abel for his ineptitude.

Abel is beside himself with recrimination and worry. How is it that his best efforts are inadequate? Again he berates himself for mediocrity, for slackness. But when this sick man dies, Abel has a dream:

There is another sick man in his bed; and the sick man also turns to him for help. In response, Abel prepares syringes with morphine and other painkillers which he administers until the sick man falls into a coma. And this time Abel does not sit nervously at the sick man's bed fearing the worst - he sits expectantly, even confidently. He sits willing death to come quickly and put the sick man out of his misery. For no amount of care or medicine can save him! And Abel sees himself smiling when the sick man opens his eyes, and seeing the host beside him, calm and at peace, announces that he is ready to die; it will be better to die than to live fearing death and hating his wretched pain-giving body.

Then Abel, watching the sick man rise from the bed, observes that the sick man has his own features, his build. Indeed, the resemblance is startling. And the two men smile at one another. They go out into the world. The sick man seems wholly cured. He walks with a bounce in his step, a self-satisfied look on his face; and Abel, proud at his side, knows that all will see how well he has accomplished his mission. So they go about the town, knowing the new day will bring what they desire. And that evening, when the two men return to the house, they cook, eat a meal, sit afterwards by a fire. And while sitting at the fire, Abel hears familiar voices at the door. They belong to his wife and children. And he leaves the sick man and goes to greet them. They embrace, exchange gifts. But when he leads them back to the fireplace to introduce them to his new friend, the sick man has left.

*

When Abel awakes, he is not surprised. He is alone with himself. At last, he is free of worry, free of stress - at last, he has truly come home.

JOURNEY TO AND BEYOND THE BORDER

A man is on holiday. He takes an organized tour on an old-fashioned steam train. With him is a group of people he has not met before. He is reserved in his contact, but among the others there is soon a jovial almost carnival atmosphere and laughter fills the railway carriage. Meandering along, the train stops at different places - resorts spas, towns, places of interest ... And while it winds its way slowly between stops, and the group congregates in the cabins, entertaining each other, he stands alone in the corridor gazing blankly at the passing scenery: the rivers, the hills, the forests. Is this how his holiday is to be spent? He so much wants to relax and join them, but try as he may he cannot break his sense of apartness.

The journey continues; days blur. The only time he feels alive is when he visits the toilet. There on the shiny metal floor he finds two antique coins, both of which have inscriptions he presumes to be in Arabic. On one side they bear the heads of men he supposes were rulers; on the other, what he supposes are letters and numerals - the name of a province, a declaration of power; the value of the coin. The man is fascinated. He wonders where they came from, what the inscriptions mean. And though he knows no Arabic, he allows a romantic nostalgia for the time once spent in various Middle Eastern countries to uplift him - and break what he now resentfully considers the predictability of the shrill festive voices inside the carriage, the silly male/female sparring ...

He remains in the toilet for some time, studying the coins, swaying as the train rushes along. And he forgets where he is, conjuring up the richness of Mediterranean mythology and grandeur. Eventually he resumes his stand in the corridor, but the rhythm of the journey is now interrupted by frequent and lengthy breakdowns; and during these enforced periods of waiting, the fields become flatter and more monochrome, the farmhouses squatter, more monotonous . . . No explanation for these interruptions is given. The tourists are left to themselves while the train idles. And while trying to come to terms with these doldrums, he develops a sense of suffocation, of claustrophobia: stop, start, stop, start, stop, start . . . His mood becomes blacker. But his fellow passengers do not allow themselves to be affected; they continue with their animated discussions, their games and playmaking.

Then the train enters a grimy, industrial town situated near the border with another country. It reaches the central station, stops briefly and moves on, but soon afterwards halts on the outskirts of the town. Is there another train just ahead? Once again the scenery offers no pleasing or grand views. The atmosphere is smoky, grey with industrial effluent and smog. And again the man begins to feel frustrated though he knows there is nothing to be done - he must control his impatience, sit out the boredom. He tries to revive the fantasy elicited by the coins, but the images fall dully to his feet. And then, while he is standing listlessly in the corridor, staring out, he notices that people are walking past the train in the direction of the border. Tired out and shabby, some carrying small parcels, but many with nothing in their hands or on their backs, they trudge by, and he is intrigued by this exodus, although the people are remote from him, removed from his situation.

Hours pass. The train remains stationary. No one reports to them as to when they are expected to move. Even his fellow vacationers begin to loll dejectedly, their conversations falling into stale pauses. Then one of the women in the group steps out of her compartment and approaches him. She suggests that they leave the carriage and walk along the railway line to the saloon located at the front of the train. She smiles teasingly - perhaps a few drinks will reignite their enjoyment of the tour. Amazed that she should be inviting him, and surprising himself, the man accepts her invitation. She leads him to the carriage door. At last the trip is taking on a very pleasurable dimension! However, as they alight from the carriage, the train pulls off and they are left stranded on the track surrounded by the silent, raggedly dressed people streaming towards the border.

He swears in disbelief, turns to commiserate with the woman, but contradicting her earlier friendliness, she leaves him and disappears into the crowd. Angry and panic-stricken, he wonders what to do. He must catch the train before it reaches the border! He must move fast! So, without money and his passport, he slips into the flow of people, acutely aware that he has nothing except the clothes he is wearing, and that if he fails to board the train before it reaches the border, it is unlikely that he will be able to rejoin the group. He grits his teeth, pushes on at a faster pace. The stream of people is soon overshadowed and overtaken by convoys of military trucks, armaments and other official vehicles. With growing horror he realizes that they are refugees and that he is in a country at war and will have even more problems without official papers.

Night falls. He reaches a signpost. Beyond it, standing next to a boom, a passport control officer dressed in a white uniform with gold epaulets, blocks the narrow path leading to the border. Choking with fear, the man approaches. The officer challenges him. In a quivering voice he explains that his tour group is on the train that has just passed, and that he wishes to rejoin them. The officer looks at him suspiciously, but after a few moments raises the boom and waves him on. Not daring to look back, he quickly crosses into no-mansland; the mass of people pass with him, all of them trying to project confidence. And there, beyond the boom, they reach the outskirts of an abandoned village.

The houses are in a state of disrepair. Large brick and mortar structures with balconies and embellishments such as turrets and cornices, wrought iron railings and blinds, they are draped with seaweed that hangs from the roofs and doors so that all of them are stained a yellowish-brown and give off the appearance of an underwater city. He admires the aesthetic that maintains their presence, their old-world charm and solidity. And after passing many such houses along the dusty path that runs through no-mans-land, he finds himself at the far end of the village and in front of the neighbouring country's border post.

He stops. The old fear resurfaces. Will the control officer allow him to cross without a passport? But this time he strides purposefully towards the boom, and just as he reaches it, looks down at his hand. Tucked into the sleeve of his jacket is a document. He opens it. His name and date of birth are inscribed on the inside page. Triumphant, he raises the document in the air. Without hesitation the passport officer lifts the boom and waves him through. Then he hurries to find the group. He recalls that their first excursion in the neighbouring country was to be at a ski resort. And after several hours of hiking along mountain roads, he sees a clump of buildings nestling in the snow. There, dotted between the buildings are human figures.

He feels a thrill of recognition - he will soon resume the tour, but this time he will not stand alone, he will become part of the whole, he will sit and talk and joke with everyone.

He knows he will finally begin to enjoy his holiday.

WAR TIME

"That which you have done - whether it be only once in your life, in one moment of stupidity or in an outburst of anger - that which you were capable of doing - even if you have forgotten, or have chosen to forget, how and why you did it - that which you have done and regretted bitterly, you may never do again. But you are capable of doing it. You may do it. It is curled up inside you." Amos Oz

1

It was the third year of the civil war. Our country was divided; the cities controlled by opposing armies. My brother and I were still young boys. We lived out a daily struggle, most times scared and hungry, only surviving by breaking into abandoned buildings and scrounging things to trade for food.

At the beginning of the war, our father, like most of the family, had joined the Greens. He was stationed in our hometown, but after a few months he was transferred to another province and we were left alone with our mother. The war intensified. The Green army moved into Blue territory. The battles were fierce; there were heavy casualties on both sides. However, despite our fears for his safety, we received encouraging news from our father, and lived in hope of victory and his safe return. Then the Blues counter-attacked and captured our city. Contact with the outside world was cut. Food was difficult to find and services collapsed. Deportations began. We lost contact with our father. Only our mother's great courage and resourcefulness saved us. Day after day she would leave our home, forage and bargain. But then, several weeks after the start of the occupation, she did not return.

We searched where we could, made enquiries. But no one recalled her; no hospital or morgue reported her presence. Our fear grew that she was dead and had been secretly buried, or that she was a prisoner of the Blue commandos. And if that was the case, we shuddered. Our media had reported that the Blues raped the women they captured, forced them to work in arms factories; and that, as soon as these women became sick, or were unable to keep pace with the work, or were able to provide the Blue soldiers with sex, they were shot.

We hoped against hope that she had survived, that she was somewhere safe. But the days passed, and so it was, given the disappearances of both our mother and father, that we had to accept that young and vulnerable as we were, we would have to fend for ourselves.

*

One night we made a hideaway in a bombed out house. I was lying awake; my brother was sleeping. I heard two men enter the house and stand near our hiding place. Matches were struck, followed by the crackle of burning cocaine. Then I listened to them talking.

They said the war was over. The Greens had overrun the Blue capital and the Grand Leader of the Blues had gone into hiding. They said a train would arrive in our city by morning and that Green soldiers would take control - the local Blue commander had already disappeared, the rest of the occupying officials and soldiers, having burnt their uniforms, had fled into the surrounding countryside. Finally the two men spoke of their certainty that the Greens would take harsh revenge; that after the violence and butchery carried out by the Blues, there would be systematic and savage reprisals.

The conversation continued for some time. Then I heard the men's footsteps bang on the broken wooden floors and stamp out of the building. Was the war over? There had been so many rumours, but every week fresh reports of victory had proven false. And yet, despite my disbelief, my weakness and fatigue, I was filled with hope. Just imagine! Many things would again be possible if the Greens had won - our father, perhaps even our mother, could return! I woke my brother and told him what the men had said. Though it was far distant from where we were, I suggested we walk to the railway station to see for ourselves. And sure enough, just before dawn, when we finally arrived at the station, we found it crowded with men in Green uniforms.

The Green soldiers formed long lines and marched off into the city. Then they spread out into the rubble-strewn suburbs - some to bring order and seek out the last surviving enemy, others to take off their uniforms and again become civilians. What a rush of activity there was in the station! Train after train pulled in, crammed with our troops. Almost lost in the welcoming crowds, my brother and I stood on the platforms scanning the soldiers. Between arrivals we moved through the mass, searching for the face we remembered. But though we watched thousands of soldiers line up, then march off, none of them was the man we desperately hoped to find.

We waited the whole of that day at the station; we waited the whole of the next. How difficult a task it was! Though they tried to look fresh and victorious, the Green soldiers were haggard and worn out. Soon all faces blurred into a single, drained image and I began to fear that after all these years, I had forgotten what our father looked like, and that because of my faulty memory, I had passed him by as if he was a stranger. The streams of Green soldiers filling and leaving the station, ebbed and flowed, but still he did not arrive. Then, on the seventh day, I realized why we had missed him: he had changed. Of course! Just think how much he had changed! He had been so affected by the war that we could no longer recognize him. The war had effaced the man, the father, who had left us to fight. That loyal and loving man, worn down by battle, scarcity and fatigue, was now someone we could never imagine - overwhelmed, shadowed, battered by suffering, he had become another person whom we could not identify.

I shared my understanding with my brother. He listened carefully, but denied that it could be true: our father was no weakling. No matter how great the stress he had had to endure, he could not have changed to such a degree - he would still be the man we knew, his goodness would have resisted all pressures. Oh, how sure my brother was that our father had survived and that we only had to be patient!

And I allowed myself to be convinced by this argument, but, almost to spite my brother's resolve, my stomach went into spasms and I broke out in a fever.

Overcome with sorrow and physical pain, I cried out, "Hope is futile, it is time to accept his death and leave the station!" My brother stared, unsure how to calm me. And then, at that moment, while I was doubled over, the last train of the day pulled in, and our father was the first man to jump onto the platform.

He had lost much of his hair and a thick cover of stubble darkened his cheeks; otherwise he was without doubt the man we loved. My brother and I ran to him. He threw up his arms, called out our names. And we stood together, embracing, locked together, overwhelmed by an emotion greater than anything we had ever experienced: my father, my brother and I, each of us crying uncontrollably.

2

My father is bald, stooped, quite feeble. I am a mature man in the prime of my life. We are in a wood-paneled courtroom. The prosecutor rises, begins to read aloud from a thick charge sheet - page after page describe brutal crimes committed against an endless number of victims. Finally, the prosecutor comes to the end of the indictments. He closes his file. The packed courtroom is numbed, silent. How is one to respond to this chronicle of evil? How is one to deal with the perpetrator?

Slowly, carefully, the prosecutor sums up. Then he names the accused. I feel my whole being convulse. It is unthinkable! My father - a torturer, a murderer? How could this sensitive man have committed atrocities? His whole life has been built on decency, on sacrifice, on concern for his family and for others.

The courtroom, up to this point so familiar, seems foreign; the wood paneling once so attractive and comforting, seems ugly and forbidding. And the crowds of people in the gallery, though known to me in an almost intuitive way, now also seem alien - it is as though old and intimate friends abruptly began speaking a strange, incomprehensible language.

The prosecutor faces me. The judge calls out my name. My father sits very still. The judge repeats my name and I confirm that I am my father's lawyer; it is my task to represent him. Then the judge orders my father to rise and plead. I feel relieved - soon it will be time for me to lead his statement of defence. I turn to my father and wait for his calm denial; I turn to him and await his measured rebuttal of the obscene charges. But my father falters, his voice chokes and he looks down. The judge repeats his question. My father still struggles to speak. The court gallery buzzes. I grow perplexed, agitated. How can this travesty of justice be permitted to continue? How can a weak old man be subjected to such emotional torture? I stare bitterly at the judge - sanctimonious bureaucrat! What does he know of the civil war hero who defended our people so bravely? How can his good name be smeared so callously? To what end?

My father faints. The orderlies bring him water. I ask for a recess but the crowds in the gallery begin screaming, calling us names - despicable names. I turn to the judge for protection. I despise this rabid witchhunt! But when the judge again instructs my father to stand, I churn with even greater outrage: is this what we fought for - legalized victimization of the veterans who fought with such honour?

I help my father stand but he is unable to talk. The judge orders me to continue. It is clear he will show no mercy. Then, as I begin, I see that my father suddenly seems more conscious, more composed, and I am jubilant. Now we will deal with those who have so insolently thrown our lives into turmoil! I ask him to answer the judge: is he not innocent of these charges? But as I do so, the prosecutor hands my father a file.

My father stands with the file in front of him. The prosecutor opens the file.

I repeat my question. The crowd again grows restless; once more the catcalls ring out. My father lifts his eyes. He stares up beyond the judge and shakes his head. I try to attract his attention but he avoids me. The prosecutor turns page after page. My father refuses to look down at the file.

The prosecutor brings me the file. I open the file.

Photographs. Photograph after photograph. There, in all of them, my father, ashen like the dead men and women on whom he stands.

I tell the judge that these photographs have been tampered with, forged. They are a hoax. The man cannot be my father. There is no doubt that he cannot be my father.

Corpses: in forests, in town squares, on sports fields, in supermarkets, at street corners.

The man cannot be my father.

The judge declares the prosecution should bring the witnesses forward. The crowd filling the courtroom rises. One by one, they take the stand; one by one, they give their evidence. But I know it cannot be my father. Why have they manufactured these lies? Why do they persist in taunting this decent old man? Why are they showing us these doctored photographs of corpses - in swimming pools, in prison cells, in bedrooms, in schools? I face him, reassured by the memory of the joy I experienced at the station on the day he returned from the war.

Still my father remains silent.

Only later that night, when I dream, and see him hanging, do I accept that anything can become a lie.

BLACK COAT

A fresh, lovely day; I am walking by the sea along a road that winds, and winds, following bays that sparkle with sunlight. Ahead of me I see a woman in a heavy black coat. I am surprised that someone is wearing such a garment considering the sunny weather, and when I catch up to her, I turn round to see who she is. And I am overwhelmed: she has dark hair and dark eyes; burning, intense eyes; long, curly locks that frame her white face. All I want to do is fill my vision with her! However, I feel embarrassed to keep staring, so I walk on and leave her behind. Then a little while later a bus passes and I see that she is on board. I feel sad. Now I will surely not see her again! I continue walking, trying to be cheerful. After all, I console myself, the day is still light and airy and her disappearance is just 'one of those things'.

Suddenly another bus comes along, and I jump aboard - maybe I can still find her. I sit on the top deck to have a better view. An old man is also there. He is with a young boy. The old man is explaining something to the boy. I cannot hear what he is saying, but I pick up his deliberateness, his solemnity. The boy, however, finds it hard to concentrate; he fidgets, does not seem to understand. And I wonder why. Is it deliberate (a form of defiance)? Or is it that he has a learning difficulty, perhaps even brain damage that makes comprehension an ordeal? The old man soldiers on, repeating, rephrasing. However, little by little he begins to lose patience, and I feel sad that, despite his tenacity, he is being defeated by the boy's obtuseness. But then, as the bus rounds a bend, this scene is completely pushed aside: in the deep waters of a cove alongside the road, I see an enormous whale frolicking.

The whale has yellow barnacles encrusted all over its body. When it dives out of the water, the barnacles glitter and it seems bedecked in jewels. The sight is overwhelming, for the whale is very close to the shore, and so free and spontaneous and acrobatic that for a moment I think it is a man-made yellow lizard being manipulated by a film crew! I decide to leave the bus and enjoy more of the spectacle. And there, where I alight, I find a specially designed sea-viewing platform, complete with benches. Greatly pleased, I sit down to give myself up to the awesome display. The whale does not disappoint. Again and again it leaps up out of the water, its glistening hulk corkscrewing in effortless arcs before crashing back under the waves. What agility, what power! The yellow scales scintillate and I am elated. Then several minutes later I am given another eventful surprise: the woman in the black coat arrives. Looking more alluring and mysterious than before, she sits down beside me, eyes blazing, hair lustrous and shiny. And to my joy, she takes my hand (how intimate it feels!), and begins talking.

She tells me that she is a junkie, and that, right now as we speak, she is on drugs, and that she cannot control her habit. I laugh and tell her not to be defensive - I am also on drugs! We embrace, emotionally closer than ever. I certainly have no reason to feel alarmed. After all, I am united with a captivating and sympathetic beauty! Having made these confessions, we continue admiring the soaring, resplendent whale. But then, out of the corner of my eye I see two boys standing at the railing of a house set back from the bay.

The taller boy looks concerned, withdrawn, indifferent to what he sees, whereas the shorter, perhaps younger boy is gay and celebratory. I observe them with interest when a third boy appears. He is the boy from the bus and I suddenly realize that he resembles me at that age. Taken aback and wanting confirmation, I ask the black-coated woman if I am right: does this boy resemble me at that age? She smiles, squeezes my hand, replies that that is unimportant - what matters is the present. So the real question should be: does he look happy, assured? And following on from that, how do I feel at this moment?

I press her for a straight answer, but she repeats herself. Getting nowhere with her (on this issue), I leave off. But I am disappointed. For some reason it is important for me to know if this boy resembles me. As it is, my concentration has been thrown out of joint. The three boys standing at the railing overlooking the bay haunt me. Who are they? Are they figments of my imagination? Are they reconstructions from memory? Are they symbols of aspects of my own personality? And while pondering these questions, still warm with the touch of the black-coated woman, I foresee that when I reach home, I will find my son (who is more or less the same age as the three boys) in bed. And I will fix myself a place to sleep in his room and spend the night there. I also know that I will dream of this woman - so close and yet so far from me - who lives on the edge of madness.

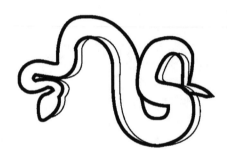

TORMENT AND PLEASURE

They had known each other for some weeks. He was taken by her but she was unsure of her feelings. However, as they were both lonely, it made sense to keep seeing one another until this ambivalence was resolved. So one long weekend they flew to another province, intending to spend a few days at a private game lodge. She was looking forward to viewing the animals as it had been many years since her last visit to a reserve. But on arrival at the airport, he informed her that he had changed the booking and that they were going to spend the weekend at 'Utopia', a nature resort he had often visited as a child. At first she was livid: how dare her undermine her preference. But there was nothing to be done, so she allowed him to have his way.

They drove away from the airport through suburban sprawl until the two towers marking the city slipped out of view and they were surrounded by well ordered fields and orchards, rows of celestial pink and blue cosmos flowers. They drove without talking, listening to Pavarotti singing Neapolitan love songs. She was still simmering with anger and disappointment. It was unsurprising that she found the songs too sentimental, and when he felt for her hand she was annoyed despite the morning freshness and the massed cosmos stalks.

The landscape changed, became more rugged - he had chosen a winding, rocky road that cut over primeval hills. When they arrived at the resort, they walked up to mountain pools filled with clear, reed-scented water and swam, then spread out in the sun. The surroundings were perfect; the earlier betrayal of her wishes began to fade. Still she was unsure whether to allow him to touch her. Then she watched him dive into the pool and his well formed body and strong strokes awoke her admiration. So much so that when she closed her eyes and prepared to doze off, it was sweet to take off her bikini top and spread out her arms, and dream that he was embracing her breasts and thighs, coaxing her into a deep, satisfying orgasm. Indeed, the dream was so luxurious that she barely felt the snake glide over her leg.

The snake slid over her as if it was a delicate finger tracing a path. She screamed; sat bolt upright. The man pulled her to him. The snake reared. The man held her tight and still. The snake swung forward, disappeared into the rock. The man smoothed her back, comforted her sobbing. Then he covered her whiteness with his brownness so that she whimpered with love and relief.

On the way back to the airport she held his hand making it difficult for him to drive, but that inconvenience was a minor problem for the road back from Utopia was empty of other cars and her hand was warm and insistent and he knew this was the start of a long and fulfilling relationship.

It was no surprise that on the plane they both proposed a toast to the snake.

ASHFORD

A woman has a baby boy. But the father of the boy leaves her and goes to live with one of her closest friends. Faced with this double betrayal, she becomes bitter and withdrawn, and some months after the father has moved out, dreams that her son will drown in the river that flows through the grounds of a school called Ashford College. The woman has never heard of such a school, but the dream is so vivid that she decides to check if it exists. In her investigation she discovers that Ashford College is a very expensive private school north of Johannesburg, and that a river, the Jukskei, runs through its grounds.

At this time she is living far away from the college, so she is not unduly concerned. But as her baby grows into a healthy and strong young boy, she begins to live in fear that somehow, despite her utmost efforts, the dream will come true. Her fear is so great that she has another dream in which she hangs a sign round his neck:

> THIS CHILD MAY NOT ENTER ASHFORD COLLEGE.
> THERE IS GREAT DANGER THERE!
> SHOULD YOU FIND HIM WANDERING NEAR IT,
> KINDLY RETURN HIM TO HIS MOTHER.

*

Years later, at the age of six, on the night before his first day at school, the boy has this dream:

It is a rainy summer morning. His mother drives him to his new school in her old car. They arrive at the ivy-covered buildings. She stops in front of a big wooden gate, gives him a kiss then pushes him out. He stands alone with his brown school case. A tall man, in a uniform, stands at the entrance. The boy hesitates, but the guard motions to him to step forward. The gate swings open. Beyond the well tended, rolling lawns, run the turbulent waters of a flooding river, the bodies of drowned people being swept along. There are also pots and pans, plastic buckets and underwear, bobbing in the torrent. The boy steps back from the gate. As he does so, he wakes up, shivering with fear.

The day after this dream, a distant uncle, with whom they have infrequent contact, arrives unexpectedly. After dinner, the uncle tells them about another of his nephews who is an excellent rugby player. The boy is in the First Team at a prestigious school. He offers to show them a photograph, takes out a copy of his nephew's school magazine. The cover shows the main entrance to a building. The security guard and the gate in the photograph are identical to those in the boy's dream.

*

Years pass. The mother becomes more relaxed; her son is older and more responsible, more independent. She has told him of her dream and warned him to keep away from Ashford College. But then, on the night of his sixteenth birthday, they both have the following identical dream:

He is hiking on a highway. A young, attractive girl of his own age driving a sports car stops to give him a lift. She tells him that she is on her way to her brother's school - a cross-country race is taking place and the prize is very valuable. She asks if he would like to enter. He is taken aback because he is not particularly athletic. But before he can respond, she removes the purple scarf that holds back her long hair, and with a smile, ties it round his wrist. He blushes and steps into the car.

They arrive at the school, drive through the imposing gate. He sees spreading lawns that lead down to a trickling stream. Several hundred runners are massed at the starting line. She gently pushes him and he joins the throng. And while he stands in the middle of the jostling boys, the girl is swallowed up in a crowd of spectators.

Then, as the pistol cracks and the runners shoot off, the dreams diverge.

*

In the boy's dream, the path along the stream is narrow and the runners are forced to bunch together. The competitors are all well trained, fit and highly motivated, the atmosphere is very intimidating. But the boy, emboldened by the purple scarf tied round his wrist, is determined to win and by the halfway mark has battled through to the front. With a quarter of the course to go, only he and one other runner remain in contention. They enter the final stage. Over the roar of the crowd, he hears the girl's voice - she calls out, urging him on. Exultant, he surges ahead. But as the finishing line comes into view, and he prepares for the final sprint, the other runner grabs the scarf at his wrist, and pulls him violently to the side.

The boy stumbles, falls to the ground. He blacks out. But moments later, when he opens his eyes, he sees that the stream's water level has suddenly risen: a flash flood is about to sweep down and overrun the banks. Instantaneously he scans the crowd. Facing away from the oncoming torrent, oblivious to the danger, the girl is still shouting support, encouraging him to get up and continue the race. He tries to call out a warning, but before he can open his mouth, the water crashes down, and he wakes.

*

In the mother's dream, the pistol is fired and the boy sets out on the race. Proud to be carrying the girl's scarf, he pushes himself furiously. However, he over-exerts himself and twists an ankle. Limping along, he cannot keep up with the other runners. He begins to sweat profusely and uses the scarf to mop his forehead. The others move well ahead. He hobbles on, greatly upset, knowing he is letting the girl down. Perspiration pours down his face. But the scarf cannot soak up the flood of sweat. He wrings out the scarf but it remains saturated. Then he loses sight of the other runners and is far from the girl, the mass of spectators. Sweat gushes down into his nose and mouth. Gasping in panic, he struggles to breathe till the flood overwhelms him. He collapses.

As the mother realizes that he is about to drown, she wakes.

Years pass. The boy finishes school and goes to university. He begins to spend nights out with young women, but his mother constantly warns him against any involvement. She argues that he will be tricked into having a child or that he will contract a fatal sexual disease. The boy, now a self-assured young man, becomes impatient with this negative, doom-laden haranguing, and stops confiding in her.

The woman he likes most is tall and has long hair. One day while visiting her home in one of the wealthy northern suburbs, he passes the triple garage where the family cars are kept. He stops, fascinated by a particularly powerful sports car. He suggests they take it for a drive. She laughs - despite her father's generous spirit, he has never before allowed her to drive this car; it is his most treasured possession, a very expensive collector's item. But the young man insists, and to her surprise, when she asks for permission, her father unhesitatingly agrees. He explains that it is because he likes and trusts the young man.

She covers her hair with a bright scarf and they set off. They take a quiet road into the countryside. She drives fast, the car performs well, accelerating, taking sharp corners with ease. Then suddenly a rattling sound comes from the engine. Within seconds a cloud of smoke pours out and she is forced to pull over. Flames rise up. The young man jumps out and throws sand onto the bonnet. He extinguishes the fire but after the engine has cooled, the car will not start. It is an isolated area and they have no means of repairing the damage. There is no alternative - he must seek help while she waits. So the young man sets off on foot. Before he leaves, he kisses the young woman on the lips. She smiles, takes off her scarf and winds it round his neck.

It is the end of autumn. Already the veld is brown and dry, the air sooty with grass fires. He makes good progress along the winding road. The scarf presses against his skin, curls snugly round his neck. It gives off the scent of her body. He inhales deeply, begins to whistle a song; forgets his anxiety about her father's car, wholly absorbed by the young woman's intoxicating fragrance.

After some time, rounding a bend, he comes upon a cluster of ivy-covered stone buildings. At the entrance is a big wooden gate with a security boom. Above the gate is a large sign: ASHFORD SCHOOL. Next to the gate stands a guard in a blue uniform. The guard greets him. The young man explains what has happened. The guard replies that he should walk to the reception office where he will find help. The young man thanks him and enters the grounds.

In front of him are thick, green lawns stretching down to a river. But there is very little water; isolated brownish puddles, broken branches and a few ripped tyres litter the riverbed. And there is no sign of an office; the buildings near the riverbank are all shut up. The young man is perplexed. Then, while he is deciding what to do, the guard sneaks up and knocks him on the head with a brick. The young man falls to the ground. Dazed and bleeding, he lies helpless. The guard goes through his pockets, but he has hardly any money. Angered, the guard vengefully grabs the scarf wound round his neck, and pulls it tight. The young man screams, kicks out wildly He catches the guard in the stomach. The guard grunts, squeezes even harder, pushes his face into a muddy puddle.

The young man cannot breathe; his mouth fills with water. The scarf is now a ribbon of fire blotting out the sky. He begins to lose consciousness. But then, with a last desperate effort, he manages to ram a finger into the guard's eye. The guard howls and loosens his grip. The young man pushes him aside, struggles to his feet, picks up a rock and smashes it down repeatedly till the guard is no threat.

There is silence. The young man sits down in a brown puddle, waits for his breathing to steady. In a few minutes he will get up and walk back down the side road to the young woman and the car. But before doing so, he will search the guardhouse and find a spanner. Later he will use the spanner to wedge open the bonnet and repair the damage. And once he has done so, they will drive off without having to phone her father for help. They will hold hands and drive deeper into the mountains.

UNLOADED RUBBISH

I am working in a factory where machines produce other machines. The off-cuts, the rubbish, are thrown into bins. One day I am tasked with emptying these bins. I take them outside to a dumpster. The dumpster is big enough for all the rubbish except for the contents of one bin. So I pick up this bin, intending to find another place to empty it. However, the options are extremely limited. In fact, there is only one possibility.

The back of the factory grounds lead onto a grassy field. I enter this field carrying the bin. But I immediately feel hesitant: I cannot simply strew the rubbish in the open - the field is clean, almost pristine; will it not be criminal to soil such unpolluted land? So I dither, unsure what to do. Then while searching for a more or less hidden, discreet place to dump the rubbish, I notice several sheep spread out on the grass.

At first I imagine they have eaten a poisonous plant that has caused paralysis. But when I touch one, I realize they are frozen. This astonishes me. More particularly because I cannot see ice around them - and there is no other sign of extreme cold having caused their condition. I examine one of the sheep more extensively. Despite its immobility it does not appear harmed; every one of its limbs and its fleece is intact. I check several others. The same is true of them. They are all perfectly preserved, suspended in time. I am upset: why have they been denied the chance to live out their lives grazing the sweet grass growing so luxuriantly in the field? Dejectedly, standing with the bin in my hand, I ponder this injustice.

A number of people now enter the field. I approach them to ask if they know what has caused the sheep to freeze. No one has an answer. More people cross the field, but still no one can offer an explanation. And though my sense of frustration and impatience reaches boiling point, I begin to accept that I cannot be too harsh on them - after all, I, too, am at a loss to explain the cause and it may well be that this phenomenon is unsolvable: no one will ever have the means to diagnose and treat their affliction

Still uncomfortable about trashing the field with off-cuts, I walk back to the factory. And as I pass through the gate, I see the dumpster has been cleared and has more than enough space for this last bin's rubbish. Greatly relieved, I empty the bin and walk back into the factory. The other workers welcome me and I rejoin production with energy and commitment. Indeed, work is totally fulfilling; the machines, though impersonal, are put to good use, and as long as there is no pollution accompanying their production, I am happy to be part of the factory - annoyed and mystified though I am by the cruel condition of the frozen sheep.

ACCIDENTS

I t is a clear, sunny day. A road winds through green hills. Abel is driving his car leisurely up the steep incline of one of these hills, at ease with himself and the verdant countryside, when he is suddenly overtaken. He has a brief, almost hallucinatory glimpse of two leather-clothed, high-booted men leaning low in unison astride a massive silver engine; and for just that instant, as the motorbike, weaving slightly, surges past, he sees sleek, black hair and smooth, white cheeks shine with health and vitality.

Abel turns his head in amazement. As he does so, a sonic boom deafens him, shakes the car window causing the frame to rattle. Then, before he has time to recover, the bike cuts in front of him and the force of its swerve creates a giant wave of air that further buffets the car and makes him gasp. Abel struggles to keep control, almost leaves the road, but while he wrestles with the steering wheel, the bike speeds away and the two men become a blur. In a matter of moments they disappear over the rise of the hill.

His initial bewilderment turns to anger. What right did they have to be so reckless? The fools! Using their machine to intimidate and overwhelm, their bravado overriding any safety concerns, utter barbarians! Abel seethes inwardly, and is further annoyed when moments later a tremendous explosion shatters the afternoon. It is astounding how his relaxed drive has again been so compromised! However, he accelerates till he, too, reaches the crest of the hill. But then, as he does so, he is forced to apply the brakes in order to take the sharp bend that abruptly cuts away to one side.

The car hugs the road. Abel eases back in his seat, prepares to once more enjoy the afternoon. Whatever has caused or been involved in the explosion has not been revealed and the hills continue to undulate inducing a renewed sense of well-being and calm. The car purrs along. He begins singing, somewhat tunelessly though with gusto. But then, after taking another sharp bend, almost a hairpin, he comes upon a gruesome sight.

Both men have been thrown clear of the motorbike. Bent and bloody, their limbs twisted into irregular, unnatural positions, they lie sprawled on the ground - perhaps dead, at best badly injured. They have crashed head-on into a wall; the high, fortress-like, white wall that circles the tangled garden of a sprawling house. Gnarled trees rise up beyond the wall, unresponsive witnesses to the mangled machine that lies on its side, rear wheel spinning in the air like an upended circus bicycle whose dancing bear has slipped off and fallen.

Abel is shocked and dismayed. Despite his still barely suppressed indignation at having his tranquil outing disturbed, it is one thing to expect or predict the consequences of the lunatic speed at which the bikers had been traveling, but quite another to actually face their bloodied bodies. No doubt the driver had miscalculated the curve of the bend and failed to turn quickly enough. But, in any event, Abel theorizes, there were many other ways in which the inevitable accident would have occurred. Even if he had managed to negotiate the bend safely, would an engine part just a little later not burnt out because the throttle was being revved beyond endurance? Or, given the nature of the biker culture to which they undoubtedly belonged, would he not have suffered a heart attack from popping too many stimulants and other drugs, and collapsed onto the steering wheel without warning? So Abel surveys the scene, these various scenarios running thought his mind, aware that whatever the cause, it is clear that their foolhardiness has led to a tragic correction, and that, because neither was wearing a crash helmet, they have both sustained serious, perhaps fatal, head injuries.

Macho thugs! Nevertheless, Abel does not drive away. Half disbelieving, he sits in his car at the side of the road. The well-formed, muscular men whose backs, thrust over the massive engine, had been so expressive of fitness, strength and confidence (they had seemed invincibly welded to the machine), were now barely alive - the one now writhing and howling, his face a bloody pulp; the other, turned away, still silent and inert. Then, while Abel's thoughts swing erratically, the screaming man abruptly jerks, rolls to the side and lies inert as the crumpled bike. In the silence that follows, Abel forces himself to think practically about the situation. Given their present condition he must surely try and assist them. But what is he to do? He does not have medical skills and the sight of blood unnerves him. As such, there is nothing he can contribute on his own; in order to save them he must seek help.

Abel drives away from the white wall hoping to find a farmhouse or a village. Fortunately, after just a few minutes, he reaches a group of buildings and pulls over, leaving his car in a parking lot. He runs into the nearest building and knocks loudly on the first door, but no one responds. He knocks again, shouts out that there has been a grievous accident, that an ambulance must be called. There is still no response. Impatient, he hammers on another door. A thin, pasty-faced man opens up. Abel tells the man what has happened. The sloppily dressed, dull-faced man nods without showing the slightest sign of interest. Then, before casually closing the door, he agrees to telephone for an ambulance. Abel is confused, resentful. His intuition tells him the man will not follow through, but desperate as he is, he waits, hoping against hope that the emergency service is, indeed, being contacted. The minutes pass. The man does not return. Abel knocks again, and this time hears faint footsteps; but though he calls out, "Where are you? Is an ambulance on the way?" no one opens up. The building remains silent. Forced to accept that no one will help, he leaves. What is to become of his mission of mercy? More than ever he wants to save the lives of the two badly injured men.

He returns to his car. Driving quite carelessly, he arrives back at the white wall and the wreck of the motorbike. However, this time he is not alone: a large crowd has gathered. People mill round the motionless, disfigured bikers. Abel parks and merges into the crowd. A voice he cannot identify booms out. In bombastic fashion, the speaker announces that one of the men has drowned in his own blood, gargled to death, and that the other had died instantaneously on impact with the wall. The speaker closes off, an ambulance arrives. Attendants wrap the bodies in blankets and load them, but the crowd continues to congregate, still fascinated by the spectacle of the twisted bike, the splotches of brain on the wall and the grass.

Abel is saddened and despondent. The futility of excess cuts him to the core. At the same time, he knows there is nothing more he can do, the matter has reached its finality. He walks away from the scene of the accident, intending to continue on his trip. But his car is not where he had parked it. He searches the area, up and down the grass verge of the road; checks behind a copse of trees clustered by the white wall; it is nowhere to be found. He grows angry. He has a well-developed sense of place and direction; it is unlikely and unprecedented that he could have forgotten where he parked! Then he begins to wonder if the shock of the accident has perhaps unhinged him, disrupted his memory.

He sits down, looks out over the rolling hills where he had been enjoying the bright, peaceful day. And he relives the moment when the boorish but immaculate bikers hurtled by, battering the air with their crude almost mocking energy, their gross sense of immortality. He is disconsolate: what a waste of life! But then Abel rises to his feet, claps his hands. Is it not far better to celebrate their youth and adventurousness than mourn? Far better to salute their vibrant impetuosity and daring than to be downcast! And he accepts with equanimity that while he was frantically banging on doors trying to find help, while he had been waiting helplessly, yet expectantly, for the sluggish, run-down man to respond to his plea, someone had been preparing to steal his car; and that while he had been absorbed into the crowd at the scene of the accident, the opportunity had been seized.

Abel sets off on foot, walks away down the winding road. As he does so, the sky darkens; black clouds mass, threatening a deluge. But he does not fear the coming storm. He feels confident that the rolling countryside will once again offer its splendour.

THE FESTIVAL

A man, his wife and his mother are visiting an arts festival. The festival is taking place in a small town high in the mountains. It is mid-winter and bitterly cold; a heavy layer of snow covers the ground. Despite the adverse conditions, many people are attending the festival, and there is an atmosphere of stimulation and excitement.

The man, his wife and his mother crowd into one of many prefabricated huts where audiences have gathered for performances and to view exhibitions. A heated discussion is in progress; the subject is the representation of the Outsider in world literature. However, despite the robust exchange of ideas, he feels bored; the points raised, though pertinent, do not touch him, no real insight into that mythical human archetype awakens his emotion; he finds the proceedings dry, academic.

He gazes round the hut. It is bare but for pot plants massed on a window ledge. The plants have a luminous almost bonsai quality. He stares at them, fascinated. Then he leaves his mother and wife and walks out of the hut into the snow.

*

The festival is taking place during a time of unrest. The central state has disintegrated. In its place old regional rivalries and hatreds have resurfaced. Caught up in the chauvinist hysteria, the town's young people support the war, and do not fear either killing or being killed. Indeed, they are dedicated to the fighting, and demonstrate loudly in all forums of the festival, proclaiming the superiority of their local culture and attacking those of their neighbours - once friends, now become enemies.

The man walks through the crowds, moving from venue to venue. In each hut a different event is taking place, but in his view they all seem shallow and vulgar, populist in form and content. Frustrated and dejected, he returns to the hut where his wife and mother have remained, and finds that they are still caught up in the discussion on the Outsider.

He opens the door. He had not been gone more than an hour or two, but he is amazed to see that in this short time his mother has greatly aged; she sits hunched over and one side of her face sags in, collapsed into a formless, hanging lump of flesh. Moreover, she, who was always so active and talkative, is now deathly silent, and stares at him beseechingly. The man is horrified. What has caused this sudden disintegration? He looks away; he cannot accept the distortion of her features and her brooding agony; he cannot bear witness to her inexplicable decline. Then he staggers out the hut, rejoins the crowds, but feeling disoriented, wanders blindly off on his own, following an ice-covered river embankment.

After some time, still in a state of shock, he reaches the far side of town. There, along the slope of the embankment, bordered by empty fields, he comes upon a row of large shrubs. A distant memory stirs him. As a student he had spent a summer in this town and participated in a campaign to plant trees and vegetation. Indeed, one of his tasks was to plant these very shrubs! How fulfilled he had been! And people had complimented him on his good work. But now he sees that all the shrubs are shriveled, quite lifeless; their once luxuriant green leaves drooping and faded.

Void of direction or desire, staring morbidly at the dead plants and the icy fields, he is at a loss for words. Then, suddenly, his wife appears, and quietly takes his arm. They stand together in the snow. He is pleased to see her, but remains downcast. He shakes his head, points to the rotting vegetation. But to his surprise, she smiles and congratulates him, says how happy she is to see that his plants have done well, look so lush and healthy. And she kisses him, praising this work of his youth. The man is shocked, and suspicious. Why is she being so tactless, so mocking? The plants are obviously diseased, remnants of once glowing organisms. Why does she caress his cheek, murmuring how proud she is of his fertile hands, his dedication, his vision? Why is she lying so crudely?

He turns away from her, bitter, his depression deepened by her charade. And then out of the corner of his eye, he catches sight once more of the row of shrubs and sees that, indeed, the leaves are green and full, the stems upright and strong. He calls out, incredulous, de- lighted. How could they have revived so quickly? He faces his wife again. She embraces him.

Arm in arm, they walk back to the hut to tend to his wasted mother.

IN THE COURTYARD OF THE ZEALOTS

M y wife, son and I are visitors to one of the Balearic Islands on which there is a large and well organized community of fund amentalists named 'Gush Emunim', the Alliance of Believers. On our first morning in the main city, while strolling down a narrow street in the ancient Jewish quarter, we notice a large crowd milling about in front of two large wooden doors decorated with bronze lions. I have a sense that something important, perhaps momentous, is happening.

I pull my wife and son towards the excited gathering. But before I can question anyone, the doors swing open and the crowd surges forward, taking us with it. Once inside, we find a large courtyard where marshals direct us to line up, then lead us to a large but squat sand-brown building. Above the entrance to this imposing building, suspended by an iron chain, hangs a scale which they claim to be an exact replica of the Scales of Justice that hung above the High Court in Jerusalem at the time of the Judges. The courtyard is wide and spacious. Neat rows of flowers run along the pathways that criss-cross it, and ornate, wrought-iron benches set at regular spaces alongside closely mown sections of lawn give added balance and weight. We gaze about, impressed by the geometrical orderliness of the design, the settled air of solemnity. And while we stare in fascination, two Moroccans are brought in under guard.

There is a buzz of excitement. Voices rise up, saying that the men are to be tried for the rape of a pious young woman, the daughter of a ritual slaughterer. The reports are conclusive, unwavering - there is no doubt as to the men's guilt. But, even as I listen to these expressions of outrage, I know with complete certainty that they are innocent of any such crime; that, in fact, the men are revolutionaries, members of a progressive underground organization that fights all forms of bigotry and violence; and that, on account of their militant actions in defense of an open society, they have been framed by the religious authorities who are now preparing to stage a show trial to justify judicial murder. I intuitively know this but I do not react.

My wife, son and I stand in the long line, waiting with everyone else to gain admission to the courtroom. The line moves very slowly. I grow impatient. Then I have an idea. I leave my wife and son and walk to the section where the judges have their chambers. There I engage one of the court officials, challenging him to provide evidence of the men's involvement in any crime; in particular one as odious as rape. I also challenge him in regard to the fairness of the judicial process. It seems the final sentence will be decided by popular sentiment. I protest that many people have been bribed to vote in favour of a guilty verdict and death by hanging. I advance my arguments carefully, but the imperious court official dismisses me with contempt. I leave feeling greatly angered; more convinced than ever that the trial will be a sham, a puppet show, a hatchet job in the service of an arrogant and ruthless power.

I rejoin my wife and son. I explain that there is no point in staying to watch a travesty of justice. We depart, and as we reach the wooden doors, a man in a black cape rushes forward and plunges the sharpened end of a steel wire into my son's eye. He screams. The attacker runs off. I am stricken, paralyzed by shock and concern for our beloved son. Then my wife and I are separated in the mad rush of people who flee from the sight of our son, whose eye spurts blood. I faint.

When I recover consciousness, it is noon. I am alone. I am lying in a small side street. I do not know where I am. My instinct is to report the attack on my son, and my wife's subsequent disappearance, to the authorities, but I fear that the island police have been bribed and work under the direction of the zealots. Instead of exposing myself to more harm by trusting them, I decide to find a lawyer who is independent and courageous. He will engage honest private detectives, will know how to handle the courts, manage the crooked judges. But where am I to find such a person? I wander round the old quarter.

It is a verdant city, fed by rain. Narrow alleys with garden terraces overlook the sea. I pray that a signboard will reveal the one I seek. I walk for hours, and though the afternoon passes without success, my hope does not die: my son will recover and my wife will be safe; somehow I will locate the right person to help me achieve this.

By sunset I reach a remote suburb. I find myself in front of an unexceptional, modest house with a worn black and white sign attached to the wall. The sign reads: *Nachum Lapidus - Attorney at Law*. Before I can ring the bell, a fleshy man in an old-fashioned, but well pressed blue suit, opens the gate. He greets me, shakes my hand with great warmth. In fluent though heavily accented English, he calls me 'Comrade South Africa'. I nod my head in acknowledgment. It seems the New South Africa is known for supporting progressive movements, has become a beacon of hope to oppressed people all over the globe.

I follow him and enter the house. Gathered inside are men and women from many different revolutionary movements. They rise and salute me as a brother. I am overwhelmed by their generosity of spirit, and thank each one in turn. Then, after a few preliminary words of introduction, I tell them of my predicament. A hum of sympathy fills the room. I wait expectantly. The lawyer calls for silence. One by one, each revolutionary explains to me that the Believers are being used by the United States government and its shadowy controllers - once again an imperial command has found Christs to crucify, once again Pharisees have allied themselves with Caesar, been prepared to do the Empire's dirty work. But then, despite their fervent protestations of support and pained expressions of regret, the comrades tell me there is nothing the lawyer or they, themselves, can do - I am on my own, the zealots are too powerful to challenge.

I am deeply distressed by their declared impotence, their reluctance to attempt any action, but I know that I cannot give up. As night settles, I leave the lawyer's house. My priority is to find my wife - once we are together, we will find our son. I continue searching despite the dim light, peering though windows, scouring the city squares. Then, after some hours, tired and dispirited, I sit down in a crowded cafe and order food and a drink. A man joins me at my table. He says he can help me. I am surprised: what does he know of my situation? But to my amazement, he knows everything - including my grave disappointment with the lawyer and the group of revolutionaries. We speak for some time. Hope is rekindled. I sense that he might be the one I am looking for, the one to offer real support.

The stranger clasps my hand. I ask him how we should proceed, and as I do so, I become aware that the other diners are furtively watching us, straining to hear our conversation - the Believers have spies everywhere. I panic, decide to leave. But as I rise from the table, a group of men burst into the cafe. Burly, rough-looking thugs, they shove me aside and rush to the wall behind our table. In seconds they rip open the decorative wooden panels. There, in a false compartment, they find an arms cache. And I am filled with dread: they will arrest me on a charge of stashing illegal weapons; I will be thrown into prison. And then with this knowledge comes the realization that my wife left me because of my showing solidarity with the accused Moroccans - for that action created the grounds for the attack on our son. She left me because I thought I could save others, but in so doing I recklessly endangered our family and caused us to pay an atrocious price.

The men advance to arrest me. I close my eyes.

FOUR SEASONS

D erek is parked at the back of the hotel waiting for security to open the gate. He switches on the radio, listens to music. A youngster walks up to the car. The youngster offers him a choice of dagga, crack or acid; he says he's also got rocks and Swazi. They talk. Derek explains why he's waiting. They discuss the merits of each drug. The youngster offers opinions on the quality of each high. Then they discuss the song being played. There is no sign of the security. Derek says he must get out and find the security. The youngster says he will go to the hotel lobby and find a porter. Derek thanks him, knowing the youngster is doing this to soften him up so he'll score. The youngster runs off; he remains in the car listening to music. After a few minutes the youngster comes back, tells him he's spoken to the porter. Derek gives the youngster R10. Another youngster walks over. He is about the same age. He has two missing front teeth. He wears a woolen cap on which is written GAUTENG; on his navy blue jersey is written LOVE ISNT EVERYTHING. They tell him they're partners.

A car drives past and the youngster who had gone to call the porter, who still hasn't arrived, runs after the car.

"See you now, mister, I'll be back, these are my steady customers."

*

Derek is in a restaurant across the way from the hotel. He orders the Special: *Cornflower Chicken Soup, Spring Roll, Sweet and Sour Chicken with Fried Rice, Ellis Brown Coffee*. A man walks into the restaurant. He sees there are no other patrons. He sits down two or three tables away from Derek and peruses a menu. Then he watches Derek reading J.M.Coetzee's memoir, 'Boyhood'. He does not know that Derek is reading the page which describes Coetzee's admiration for the blonde Afrikaans boys in his class who had long, tanned legs like Greek sculptures - beautiful and desirable boys, despite the words 'fok', 'piel' and 'poes' that spewed from their lips. A half-smile on his face, the man, who looks Coloured, and has a half-beard, maintains his bold look. Derek keeps on reading: nothing can destroy the frozen formality of even the most mobile sculpture. As he finishes the chapter, the man leaves his table, smiles, and comes up to him. He asks if he is from Jo'burg. Derek replies, "Yes, how do you know?" The man says he saw him park outside the hotel, and as he says this, Derek remembers seeing him on the patio where the drunks sit with the most battered whores on the beachfront.

The man patiently hangs round his table till Derek asks to be excused - he wants to start another chapter.

*

Derek's notebook is open on the table. He sips a beer and cleans his glasses. Dick Morton steps up to play. As he takes to the stage, lurching a little unsteadily, he catches sight of Derek and gives him the assurance that he will still be able to 'do his own thing'. Derek laughs, and asks if the guitar is tuned.

Dick Morton has an electronic orchestra backing him: strings, piano, bass and drums. His voice reverberates with artificial echo. He starts with Elton John's classic, 'Your Song', and the effect, though a little unbalanced - the strings are too high, too dominant - is not entirely displeasing. He asks Derek what's in the notebook.

"Your biography?

"No, a poem."

Dick Morton replies that he will play a poem he has written and set to music. He dedicates it to 'All the Children'. Then he asks Derek to come up and sing a song.

"Yes, if I can remember the lyrics."

*

The green/blue fringe shivers as it breaks onto the sand. Fishermen stand in small groups. Preparing their bait and their buckets, they anchor their long rods, lines swinging out into the surf, all set to reel in a fish. Derek can see them from his balcony, their bakkies clogging the pavement. Tanned or pitch black, coarse but not ugly, with a certain grace (despite the clinging smell of salt and fish gut), these men are made different by their contact with the waves and the many hours when they do not speak, but wait, watching the drifting lines, listening to the wind and noting the tide - those many hours praying for a bite, made merry with cane spirit and Coke.

Despite the distance, Derek congratulates them. Does it matter that they cannot hear him? Neither can the sirens who swim, well away from the hooks, off the breakwater. Making ready to go out for a plate of calamari and chips, Derek blesses the ocean and turns to light a last joint.

IT WAS RAINING

He slows down because it is raining and she is alone, and it is nightfall, and she looks bedraggled and lonely and defiant; he slows down because the rain makes her hair a soggy mass but shows her breasts; makes her breasts under her wet T-shirt stand out victorious.

She opens the car door, throws herself in. And then he smells her - despite the freshness of the rain and the perfume of the dark forest around them. He smells her rank, unwashed body and almost faints, but she throws herself in so quickly that he does not have time to throw her out.

She slams the door closed. He wants to throw her out. She takes off her T-shirt and tells him to drive. He stares in wonder at her breasts. The rain makes her skin glisten. He drives off. He drives. She tells him she is hungry. She tells him she has no shoes because her uncle stole them. She reaches to the back seat of the car and picks up the jersey his wife had given him. She picks up the jersey and pulls it over her head. Then she says, "You can play with me once I've warmed up."

By the time they reach the city, he repents: this is a rank-smelling, poor, barefoot peasant woman with no money and no education.

*

It was raining - he had picked her up He had wanted to pick her up. There she was in the rain. All wet. He knew it was wrong but she had stood in a wet T-shirt.

*

How long had he stared at her breasts?

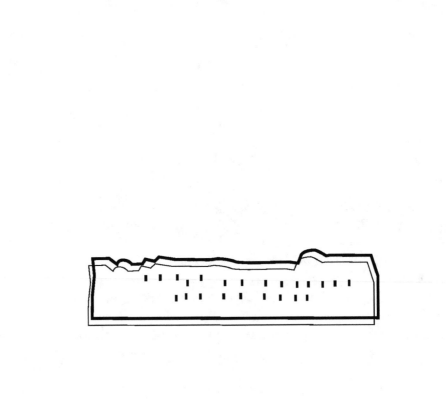

THE EDIFICE

M idday. The sun burns down on an ancient fort. Solitary in the midst of sandy wastes, it is a relic of an imperial frontier.

On the flat roof of the fort ranged side by side along its rim, a row of men on horseback mark the skyline. These faithful Warriors have survived many battles, many campaigns, are veterans of vicissitude, paragons of endurance. And their sleek, powerful horses, though dusty and sweaty, are ready to gallop into action. Indeed, they snort and paw the air. But this excitement is not capricious: it has good reason - their riders are keyed up, tense with hope and desire as they wait.

The Warriors look down. Below them, in front of the fort, alone on the parched earth, stands their Leader. Dressed as they are dressed - in a simple, white robe - he is a reluctant leader. But having accepted their ordination, he straightens his back, gazes out at what lies in front of him.

A bare stretch of ground leads down to a dry riverbed. Beyond the riverbed a hill, dotted with cacti and long grass, rises up. And his eyes pour over this desert landscape, until finally, they rest on the summit upon which stands another ancient structure.

The Leader looks up at this edifice with intense concentration. Despite the haze caused by the glaring sunlight, he notes that the building is similar to the fort behind him, and shows signs of dereliction. Had both had been overrun by an enemy and despoiled? Yet, as he studies its pockmarked, flat roof, and confirms its ordinariness, its ugliness, he sees a glow: an unshakeable, steady evanescence emanating from within the walls. And this glow pulses in proportion to his awareness of it.

The Leader breathes in deeply. He feels the current. And then drawing on this power, absorbs the individual, and yet collectively shared, hopes and needs of his followers - the patient, disciplined horsemen grouped behind him on the parapet of the ancient fort. Welling with their faith, their demand that he lead them, he knows it is time to act.

He makes his way down the slope. He crosses the riverbed. And as he begins walking up the hill towards the glowing light, the line of Warriors, as one person, urge their horses forward. They fly down from the building in a single flowing wave. And the Leader ingests this surge of energy. It fills him with both fear and exaltation - fear that he might fail to deliver them from their suffering, exaltation born of their trust in him.

The moment of union passes. With light, easy steps the Leader springs over the cacti, then rises up off the earth and lands safely, gloriously, on the ramparts of the glowing edifice. The abandoned fort, so solid, airy and bright, is now their temple. He has not failed his followers; he has not failed himself.

THE DOLL

A bel travels with his family to the Holy Land. On arrival, they reach a small village ringed by imposing purple and brown mountains, and find lodging in an old house with many rooms and a luxuriant garden. Abel marvels at the mountains. He is reminded of his first visit, many years before, when he was a young boy. Then, too, he had been greatly affected by their richly layered, sombre textures and the deep, straw/yellow valleys beyond them - a world drenched in colour, exuding the grandeur of a master artist's painting.

Abel and his family settle into the house. They sleep deeply, appreciating the austere but comfortable surroundings, and in the morning, refreshed, sitting together, they enjoy a simple but tasty breakfast. After eating, Abel kisses his wife, son and daughter and walks out into the garden.

It is a still, bright day. He hears the warble of a little yellow bird, the slight murmur of wind in the trees; he watches a chameleon turn on a branch, centipedes crawl between grass stalks. And he sighs with pleasure, feeling very full and complete, attuned to the garden, the rambling vegetation and insects, supremely aware that the human eye and heart are at most times only dimly aware of the patterns, the processes, that form and take place around us; yet every plant and creature exists for itself and for all things, striving to find its optimal expression.

Elated, Abel walks in the garden, breathing deeply and easily. How fortunate that they have come on this pilgrimage! And, in the course of this walk, he comes upon a small, bare stage. The stage, exposed to the sky, its front pointing towards the purplish mountains, stands in an opening between trees. Roughly built, white paint cracked and peeling, it is nothing more than a weather-beaten surface of dark wood. Intrigued and attracted to it, Abel decides to rest near it on the grass. And while he relaxes, contemplating this unexpected addition to the wild plant orderliness, a woman walks towards him. She is tuning a guitar.

He is taken aback; the garden has been so peaceful and he had welcomed its atmosphere of remoteness. Such an intrusion is typical of his congested hometown where no place affords quietness and privacy! Then, as the woman comes closer, he sees that her style of dress marks her as a countrywoman. And this further incenses him: the Holy Land should not be cheapened by the familiar - he has so much looked forward to losing himself in its other-worldly distinctiveness.

The woman continues walking in his direction, tuning the guitar, immersed in the activity, testing each note, each string. Still upset by her presence, he follows her progress across the garden. Then, to his surprise, he recognizes her - yes, she is from his homeland, and she is well known for her good deeds: she helps the poor and the destitute with humility, gives of herself without self-righteousness. So Abel is comforted; her identity changes everything. Indeed, he now accepts her arrival with good grace and is disappointed when she walks past him without saying a word, and makes her way to the stage.

She begins playing. The music is enchanting. Abel completely forgets his initial discontent. He draws in her beauty, is filled with such fullness and contentment that he is inspired to accompany her. He fetches a guitar from the house, returns to the grassy place in front of the stage. Suddenly, another man appears, a poet, also from his homeland. The poet, too, has a guitar. They sit together listening to the woman's exquisite song. How wonderful to have been joined by two such pure and creative souls! What more idyllic setting than this wild and perfectly balanced garden!

The two men pick up their guitars, and once each string is tuned, the poet rises, indicates that they should join the woman on stage. Abel smiles in agreement. Yes, let them make harmonies! But while they are making their way across the grass, he sees a full moon slowly mount the clear blue sky. He is incredulous. It is not quite noon. How can the sun at its zenith be paired with an equally bright moon? He looks at the poet questioningly, but the poet averts his eyes.

They reach the foot of the stage. Soon the musical communion will begin. But as they step onto the weathered floor, the woman hastily turns her back on them, hurries away. Both men are stunned when she disappears into the nearby undergrowth. What has caused her to leave? Have they offended her by assuming she would want them to join her? Does she feel they are not worthy enough to make music together, are somehow inferior, tainted? Abel is unsure whether to feel insulted or appropriately chastised. Nonetheless, despite their disappointment, the poet lifts his arm as if to conduct, and Abel prepares to play. But once more there is a disruption

In the distance, high in the air, they see a large, shiny, flying object. The poet drops his hand. There is a tense, heavy silence in the garden. The men are immobilized, intrigued if apprehensive. What is this glinting apparition that flies so fast, that seems so alien? The garden, with its luxuriant, tangled, aromatic vegetation begins to hum. The projectile, rapidly losing height, draws closer till they make out that it is a large, winged, brightly painted wooden doll.

The two men watch the doll thrust through the air at great speed. In a matter of seconds it appears directly overhead. The earth trembles, the doll vibrates, and they know that out of the clear, blue sky of the Holy Land, they are being visited by an angel. Then, as the glittering visitation rushes down towards them, standing firm, the hair rising on his neck, Abel steadies his guitar, and strikes the first resounding chord.

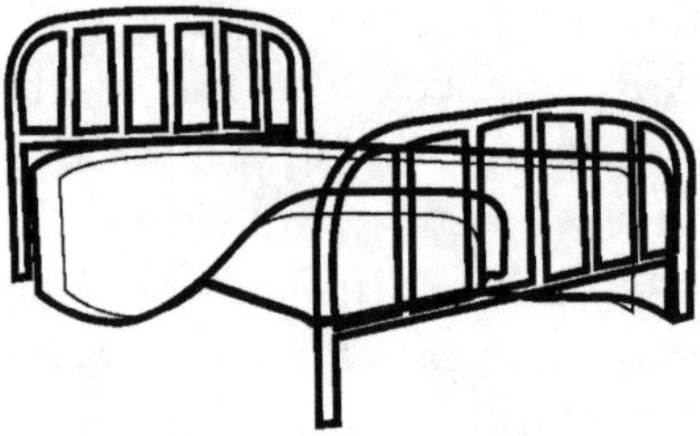

SECOND CHANCE

Victor is with his first love, Miriam. It is many years since their separation. The imbalances caused by his restless need for the bodies of other women and her psychic and emotional crises had torn apart what had been a strong and vibrant bond. How many careless days had they spent on the bed in their small flat facing a rock garden, her head on his chest, fused together, listening to Beethoven or Bob Dylan, sitar music or Congolese Missa Lubas? Yes, they had known a powerful first love. And now, for the first time since their breakup, they are together, having coffee in her apartment (in what is for him a foreign city), and he can appreciate her ever bountiful smile and her exuberance flowing towards him in waves. How her eyes reach into him!

Miriam has black hair (which, though probably dyed, still suits her) and her face is smooth and milky, remarkably unlined for a woman approaching fifty - particularly taking into account the torment of much of her life. Victor looks at her tenderly. After so many years apart they have, quite by chance, met again and it feels so natural, so comfortable, to be in each other's company. His memory returns to the last time they had been together.

They had sat at a sidewalk café, just weeks after she had been released from hospital, and though it had been a warm summers day and she had been at ease, he had been painfully aware of the consequences of her breakdown, her depression, as well as the new lines on her face and sagging shoulders that showed how much still weighed her down. Now, twenty years later, this new-old Miriam tells Victor that she works at an embassy on the days that her psychiatrist believes she is able to manage the needs of daily life, more especially the kind of interaction with other people which is almost entirely on an official, bureaucratic level.

Victor is surprised. That a psychiatrist decides on her movements, sets the daily parameters of her activity, may be true - he instinctively feels her to be utterly frank and trustworthy and that there is no chance of her consciously misleading him. But her bearing as they speak is so assured that it is difficult to understand why she would still be seeing one; in particular, one who would play such a central, if not dominating, role in her life. However, notwithstanding this doubt (or is it more a hesitation?), holding her hand, Victor knows that he is supremely fortunate that their lives have intersected again, and that he greatly wants to spend the night with her. Moreover, he senses that she, too, wishes him to remain. And this being the case, one would assume that Victor would be both relaxed and excited, knowing they would soon re-experience their intimate love-making. But, instead, he finds himself in a dilemma of which he is slightly ashamed.

The problem is that his bag is at his hotel and if he stays with Miriam he will be unable to change into clean clothes in the morning, and to wear soiled ones is unthinkable. Indeed, there is no doubting the necessity of having fresh clothes for the new day. So he continues listening to her intently, but with a growing sense of this fundamental conflict. And while reflecting on her beauty - he so much wants to stay and share her bed - a young, naked boy materializes out of the air. Victor stares at him, fascinated. Is this the child he and Miriam aborted? Their agreement to terminate her pregnancy had been spontaneous and mutual, for as students, neither was in a position to become a parent. The boy plays, unmindful of them. And Victor experiences a strong sense of regret. The abortion might not have been the right thing, after all; indeed, neither of them has subsequently had children. But when there is a knock at the door, and Jan Marius, an old friend from student times, walks in, the apparition of the naked boy disappears, and he is diverted from this wistful meditation.

Jan Marius embraces Victor, greets Miriam then talks enthusiastically about the recording Victor has recently given him (Victor is a singer and has composed many songs). Jan Marius compliments him on the production. He mentions that he has a music industry contact who is also very impressed and would like to meet him, and perhaps conclude a deal to do another recording.

Victor glows with pleasure - he has battled for many years to win financial backing for his music projects. This turn of events is most gratifying.

The two men shake hands and Miriam smiles.

*

A few days later, Victor is on a train returning home. A squad of soldiers is also on the train; they are short, stocky, tough-looking men with heavy beards.

The train has just crossed the border. Victor sees a procession of people walking back towards the border post. And as the train travels deeper into his home country, the soldiers grow more and more unkempt, noticeably unwashed, gaunt, and the scenery fills with stunted trees, stumps and sparse vegetation.

The train enters a tunnel, a narrow crack in the mountain. Unconsciously, Victor bends; he feels claustrophobic as the train descends underground. He sighs. Why had he not spent the night with Miriam?

The duck paddles in the pond

THE BEAUTY OF INTELLIGENCE

The afternoon was nearing its end. The boy sat on the sofa watching television. His father entered the room with a cup of milk.

"Here, my boyo. Not too hot, not too cold." The boy did not respond. "What do you say, kiddo?" Totally absorbed, the boy still did not respond. "Isaac . . . I'm waiting." The cartoon figures screeched and sped all over the screen. "Isaac, I'm waiting! Here's your milk."

"Ok . . . ok, dad." The boy seized the cup.

"And what do you say?" The man stood next to the sofa. "Hmm?" The boy continued to watch the screen. "Isaac! What's up?"

"Dad, I'm watching! Can't you see? This is the best part! Wow, look at that . . ." He jumped up then collapsed back onto the sofa, almost spilling the drink.

"Hey! Careful!" The man shook his head. "And where's the magic word?"

"Wait, dad!" The boy pointed at the television. Then an advert broke the action. He mumbled, "Ok," and shook his head sulkily. "Tha . . .ank you, dad." He broke off, the mumbling dying, even as he smiled when the cartoon flashed back on again.

"Please, boyo. It's time for homework. Switch off the tv and fly to your desk. That favourite program of yours ended about half an hour ago." The man clapped his hands. "Come, my love, let's get it out the way so we can both relax. Come, my boyo!"

But the boy squirmed and continued watching, fascinated by the images, the music, the squeaky, hyped up voices, the cutting humour and its violence.

"Isaac, I'm not speaking again!" The father stood above him, waited. "Right, you leave me no choice. I'm going to have to suspend your monthly present. Ja, that's it, kiddo . . . I'm going to have to punish you, Isaac. You're leaving me no option because every day now for the past three weeks you've made doing homework a massive bind. It's really upsetting our lives. We fight every afternoon. What's up? It doesn't take that long, and even if it's sometimes difficult, you're learning, you're getting better at it. Why turn it into such a fuss?"

"I'm no good at homework, dad! You know that! I can't do anything properly."

"Nonsense! I like the stories you read. And the ones you make up! Even your spelling's improved . . . well, sort of." He ruffled the boy's hair. "Look at it as a game - putting a puzzle together."

"But we do the same stuff everyday! And why do I have to do extra? It's not fair!"

"No, we don't do the same stuff everyday. It may seem that way, but I switch the words around. Of course, we have to come back to the same ones sometimes, but that's because you have to build your knowledge, my love. Step by step. That's how we all learn." The man touched the boy's arm. "Miss Elle said it will help and it has. You're improving everyday."

The boy looked down. "I still can't read properly."

And he was right. He was struggling. Week by week, he had grown more despondent, concentration slipping as each new assignment taxed him more than the last, until this morning when the teacher had asked him for the hundredth time to be quiet and stop disrupting the other children, he had made a rude sound, and during the break, for the first time since he had been at school, started a fight. Neither he nor the other boy had been hurt, but the incident had been ugly and the principal had phoned the father to express concern.

"Isaac, I'm switching off the tv." The father walked towards the television. "Please come, my love." The boy jumped up, and ran out. "Good! Now let's get down to it!"

The father switched off the television and went to his son's bedroom. A small desk took up one of the corners. Above it was a cluster of butterflies; they were pinned to a card. Next to the butterflies was a map of the world, and above that a photograph of leaping dolphins.

"Let's see what you've got today." The boy took out his homework book. "By the way, on which day do you have swimming? Is Ms. Seale still taking you? I hope so."

"No. Not this term, dad. We've got Mr. Walrus." They both laughed. The boy sucked the end of a pencil and opened the book. "We've to make sentences with these words. Then we have to write out those words." He pointed to pictures of various objects. "Then we got numbers."

"What should we start with?"

"Come on, dad, you know! It's always spelling. Boring old spelling!"

And the boy, without further fuss, handed his father a sheet of paper on which the words were set out.

"Right . . ." the man scrutinized the page, "spell FROG. Huh, that's an easy one." The boy scrawled f-r-o-g. "Spell ADVENTURE." The boy wrote a-d-v-e-n-c-h-u-r. The father leaned over and shook his head, but continued. "Now spell EXCITING." The boy grimaced but quickly wrote e-x-s-i-t i-n-g. "Pretty close, well done. Right, last word . . ."

"Wait, dad, let's leave it till after I've done my sentences."

"Why? Let's finish one thing at a time, then we know it's done and we can carry on without worrying that we'll forget to come back to it." The boy always wanted to cut corners, avoid completing the work at hand. But the father kept calm. "Fine, let's do your sentences, but we are definitely coming back to finish the spelling - no arguments, right? There's just one more word."

"Thanks dad!" The boy smiled. And without further comment began constructing sentences.

"For 'paddles' I'm going to write *The duck paddles in the pond.* How's that, dad?"

"Good, very good." The father touched his shoulder affectionately and the boy continued to make up sentences with several other words, the father complimenting him when he was right and gently correcting him when he was wrong.

"There we go! That was easy! We've finished with sentences. What's next?"

The boy turned to his reading, a new book from the library - a chapter had to be read aloud.

"Must I start?"

"Of course, the way we always do it. Start with the title and the name of the writer."

The boy read: "THE GI . . . ANT AND THE . . . SACK ... OF SAND by An .... dy Smith .... A cru . . . el and gree . . . dy gi . . . ant live . . . d a . . . lone in the fo . . . rest. He lo . . . ved many ....things but . . . the thing he . . . lov....ed most was .... gold. He had an . . . enor . . . mous sack ... full of gold. One day a . . . poor ... boy came to the gi ... ant's h ... ouse."

The father, sighing as the boy wrestled with the words, caressed his cheek. "Isaac, sound out every letter first. Then put them together." He gave a quick demonstration. The boy nodded and began to sound out each letter, but his progress was slow.

"When the gi....ant was slee . . ping by the fire, the boy too...k two gold co...ins from the giant's sack and cr...ept away. A few days la . . .ter he came back. He told the gi....ant that he had ma....gic sand and that this sand cou...ldn't . . .tu .. .rn to. . . gold." He stopped, put the book down. "Dad, can't we do this after supper? I'm really feeling tired, my head's all buzzy."

The boy rubbed his temples, but the man shook his head, and the boy morosely picked the book up again.

"Last bit. Ok, dad? Then can we play soccer?"

"Deal!" The father put out his hand and the boy slapped it. "Let it roll!"

"He then invi . . . . . . ted the gi . . . ant to . .test the sand. The . . gi . . . ant put one gold coin into a sack of ma . . . gic sand and fou . . .. nd th . . . ree. The boy then as . . . ked the gi . . . ant to put ano . . . ther two gold co . . . ins into the sack. The ne ...... xt day the gi . . . ant f......ound six . . ."

Little by little, the story unfolded, and the boy became engrossed. The father sat quietly as he battled with the words, sounding them out, twisting them, sometimes mangling them, but slowly, determinedly, starting to find a rhythm, a wave of fluency. Page by page, the sack of sand became gold and the boy laughed to learn of the trick that outwitted the greedy giant, he laughed in admiration of the resourceful boy who could outsmart him. And that afternoon he read more than he was supposed to - he read the whole book before setting it down on the desk under the leaping dolphins.

"That was a story, dad!

"Yes, Isaac. That was a very clever story and you read it beautifully." The father kissed his son. "Now guess the last spelling word?"

"What is it, dad? How do I know? You've got the list."

"Yes, I've got the list, but you help me make it." And he paused, but not from doubt. "Write, CE .. LE .. BRA . . ."

INVESTMENT

The Young Unknown Poet had the good fortune to publish a slim debut volume. Even greater good fortune brought him three reviews (all of them favourable) and for him, as an impecunious scribe, a not inconsiderable advance payment besides royalties. The poet was gratified; his estimation of his work as being equal to, nay superior to that of any other living poet on the planet, swelled to greater proportions. And so, though poetry was viewed as an obscure and irrelevant art form in his impoverished country, he strutted through the streets of the small bohemian quarter, sat puffed up at the only artist's cafe, never paid for his drinks and was careful to drop in on acquaintances just before dinner.

The months went by; the now Young Known Poet maintained what he felt to be a steady output, even reviving some older pieces for inclusion in a second book. But sadly (as is often the case), despite the relative acclaim granted to the debut volume, the publishers, upon checking sales, reported that a considerable loss had been incurred and were reluctant to go ahead with a second. The Young Known Poet was depressed, indignant. How could they put crass concerns ahead of artistic integrity? Surely they could see that his genius would bring great fame to their benighted country and that a second volume would be an astute investment in his future commercial success - to be doubly assured on publication of his timeless epic detailing the saga of the Royal Family's ancestors. But the publishers stuck fast to their position, and he was thereafter only able to publish in slim magazines that enjoyed limited circulation - of course without payment.

What was he to do? The sacred Muse still flooded him with rapture, but she neglected to feed him bread, never mind jam, and being well nigh unemployable, besides finding the task of job seeking soul-destroying and demeaning, he began to waste away. However, one day, in the depths of his humiliation and resentment, a tabloid required a reviewer of pulp fiction and pulp films and his name was mysteriously recommended.

*

Month after month, the Young Known Poet churned out the required number of reviews per the formula demanded by the editors. And month after month, he enjoyed a readership of hundreds of thousands who eagerly devoured his stirring evocations of the lowest common denominators that mass culture (as served by the global entertainment industry) could offer. However, despite his descent into the worlds of stock and crass imagination, he still penned verses that were profound and stirring and continued to imbue him with a sense of self-worth. So he lived, by day writing trashy prose that was acclaimed, by night fashioning poetic masterpieces that were ignored.

This state of affairs continued for several years. But then, two things happened concurrently: the newspaper that employed him shut down as unexpectedly as the reviewer's job had first presented itself; a number of his poems were selected by a famous foreign publisher for a prestigious anthology.

The currency of this publisher's country was worth a good deal. The modest advance and royalties offered came to an amount only dreamt of in our now Not-So-Young Known Poet's motherland. So despite his unemployment, he was well satisfied: for the second time in his life he would earn a respectable income from his real passion and finally his genius was being recognized on the international stage.

The foreign publisher duly brought out the anthology and the Not-So-Young Known Poet was singled out for the excellence of his work. Again he basked in his success though the critical acclaim was restricted to academic journals; again he visited the bohemian cafes with head held high. And some months later, obeying the law that 'success breeds success', he was invited to participate in a series to be released by another publisher; this time a small local publisher that depended on grants from the national arts council and foreign cultural funds. The publisher was trying to revive interest in the literature and arts of his country, and produced books reflecting the varying cultures and languages of their society. It was proposed to publish the work of ten poets, both known and unknown. Each poet would have an equal number of pages for his or her work, as well as the freedom to select the poems that would be included.

A meeting was convened to discuss the project. The other nine poets endorsed the proposal enthusiastically - the exposure would be substantially greater than anything that they had ever experienced for the budget made an allowance for marketing, which included launches at bookshops, television and radio interviews, as well as luncheon invitations from well-heeled corporate madams with an appetite for the spiritual. From being a marginal literary form, there was a chance to break into the mainstream. However, our Not-So-Young Known Poet did not agree.

In strident tones he observed that the design and layout used by the publishing house was stale and self-consciously avant-garde, and that its idea of including illustrations and photographs would not work as the intellectual public did not want the Logos sullied with coarse visual images. But, in particular, our Not-So-Young Known Poet was irked by the fact that in lieu of payment each poet would only receive a certain number of complimentary copies. Righteously inflamed, he demanded payment up front. And when it was pointed out that the small group who ran the publishing house was made up of volunteers (who would not be remunerated), he was unmoved. Why should poets as finely tuned and significant as he, have to suffer exploitation? Let the state coffers be opened for the country's men and women of letters! A country that does not celebrate and pay its artists is hardly worthy of respect! So he thundered, demanding that the publishing house raise at least four times the amount they had raised. And when the conveners gently explained they could not, he denounced them as acting in bad faith, and bewailed the fact that he had been brought to the meeting under false pretences.

There was silence. The other nine poets covered their eyes. The conveners apologized for having inconvenienced him and the Not-So-Young Known Poet left the meeting - although, because it was raining, he did not forget his jacket, gloves or umbrella. As he walked back to his house, he lamented their pig-headed arrogance. How could they imagine he would allow himself to be used? He was a lauded, international poet, not some local hack who was unknown and desperate for publication. Oh, no - he would never allow such people to make a fool of him and devalue his writing! History would show them!

*

The years passed. And though a few insignificant magazines published his work from time to time, our now Aging Known Poet did not succeed in publishing another volume. Indeed, embittered by this churlish ignorance and ostracized because of his resulting misanthropy, he died several years later from a burst ulcer. However, it was of course entirely predictable that, shortly after his untimely death, the publishing house which had brought out the historic series (referred to earlier), gathered his work together after securing permission from his brother (who was a refrigerator repairer and the literary executor of his modest estate), and published a monumental collection of our now Deceased Known Poet's work.

This collection was very well received and its highly profitable sales enabled the publishing house to produce three other books, one of which was the immortal classic, 'Red Eye' by Mandla Segodi, a biographical fiction based on our Deceased Known Poet, being an epic of bohemian life in the colonies that established the continent as the home of a new style that swept the world. Needless to say, the film version also did very well, and his brother, who had never read a line of his poems, profited handsomely; to such an extent that he managed to send his four sons to university in the reigning empire with the result that his eldest became a professor of literature and specialist in his uncle's oeuvre, becoming quite famous for a most erudite analysis of the Mask as a cardinal image in the now Acclaimed Deceased Poet's work.

This same son sired a daughter who specialized in gender studies and became notorious for her rebuttal of her father's work, and exposure of her uncle as an unregenerate misogynist and homophobe; not to mention her uncovering of his letters to a Steers cashier to whom he had dedicated volumes of rambling amorous entreaties that far exceeded his lofty philosophical poetic production. Later, of course, her daughter became a purveyor of borderline satire and made her mark by publishing the unexpurgated versions of these letters as well as a new batch of notes she discovered after secretly exhuming his grave. A third, and even more compromising batch (hidden in her mother's shroud) had been fortuitously discovered by a funeral parlour attendant who had brought them to her with the hope of making a quick buck, and succeeded.

Sadly his great-granddaughter was unable to discover the secret Sufi poems also hidden in her mother's shroud; the funeral attendant, in his excitement at massaging her cold breast and finding the first batch, had overlooked the far more suspicious bulge under her left. These sacramental, meditative works and sections of tantalizingly clipped, though multi-layered, prose texts were to lie unread for another thirty years until a great-great-great-grandson stumbled across them in the library of a school for delinquents in another continent. This descendent had emigrated after the revolution in his and the Acclaimed Deceased Poet's home country had stripped all businessmen of their property and driven out parasitic intellectuals.

The Sufi poems, written on a variety of unexpected materials - ranging from brown paper bags to plastic lunch wrappers - were to lead to a radical re-evaluation of the now Tarnished Deceased Poet with the result that his once celebrated name was restored with greater glory than ever before, and he was revered as an inspired mystic who had utilized an outer shell of pornographic imagery and offensive stereotyping to camouflage a most tender and insightful appreciation for women in particular and gay people in general.

The result of these successive discoveries - theorizing and counter-theorising - was that some time in the following century the now Rehabilitated Acclaimed Deceased Poet's estate received an enormous sum in the form of delayed royalties for the use of his Sufi poems as lyrics by a 'garage' band, being in that time an orchestral group numbering two hundred players and featuring laser inspired electronics. All this goes to show that humble beginnings and megalomania may not be impediments to long-term success.

TWO WORLDS

A multitude of people gather in a large hall. Men and women lie down, side by side, on mats. All perform yoga exercises or meditate, and fill the hall with their calm energy and a deep, complementary silence. I, too, am there; but I am not one of those transcending stress and confusion. I stand alone, an observer, interested in, but set apart from the disciplined, enlightened acolytes. And while scanning the hall, I see a large, well-built man leave his mat and sit with his neighbour - a lithe black woman who is engaged in meditation.

The man begins to fondle her breasts. She resists, moves his hands away, but he continues to fondle her. The man grows excited, pushes her down. The woman twists and turns, but he persists; he will not leave her. I watch with incredulity. How can the man be so obtuse? Of equal concern is that no one around them pays attention, and no one, including myself, intervenes. And I am dismayed at my failure to act, but to my shame, admit that I fear getting involved - the attacker is well built and I sense he would react very violently if approached. The bizarre and silent duel continues: he relentlessly pawing her, she trying in vain to restrain him. Eventually she manages to push him away, and run to one of the exits. No one around her stirs, no one moves to comfort or assist her. And I am jubilant at her escape though anxious that he will pursue her and cause her more harm. He rises; I hold my breath. But fortunately all he does is watch her leave then return to his own mat. The hall is again a mass of peaceful, reclining figures.

I give thanks, but I am still shaken. How obscene that the man had forced himself on her! And with such impunity! How could he have dared violate the spirit of the assembly? I try to calm myself. The interruption, jarring as it was, should not obstruct me from opening myself to the collective vibrations of harmony. And, indeed, after a short time, I manage to settle down; begin to re-enter the hallowed mental space. The hall hums with positive energy. My restlessness abates. So it is with doubled incredulousness that I watch him again leave his mat, and this time, turn his attention to a white woman sitting quietly in front of him. The previous scene repeats itself: the man overpowers the woman, grabbing at her breasts, forcing his hand between her legs. But though the woman's face shudders in revulsion, becomes contorted in fear and outrage, she does not offer any resistance, and he does with her what he will.

Once more I am overcome with a sense of impotence and self-loathing, and the people meditating around them remain oblivious. I scream inwardly. Why am I allowing this monster to intimidate me? But my body cringes at the thought of his power. He will beat me. I am not brave enough to intervene. The minutes pass; the molestation continues till the white woman begins to sob, and he momentarily relaxes his grip so that she is able to crawl to her feet and limp away. This time I am pleased to see that a man in a white coat, perhaps a doctor, comes to her side and ushers her out of the hall.

The attacker returns to his mat. He lies down, as if nothing has happened. Surveying the lines of peaceful men and women, still absorbed in their uplifting exercises, I am again stunned and depressed. How cowardly that I, and they, allowed these women to be violated? And I regard the attacker, now going through the motions of meditation, with vast suspicion. When next will he strike? When next will he assault, and in so doing, again confront me with my fear?

Then I ask myself if I should not leave the hall, so that I do not have to be a witness. Should I not leave to mourn my weakness? I ask these questions, admitting everything, but I am unsure, so I remain, shaking my head sadly. Truly, I do not know what to do. I have betrayed the defenseless, and until I build up my strength and courage, I will have to live with my shame.

KNOW/YES

They live in a gated suburb. He is an asset manager, buys up stock options and monitors investment returns; mocks those who suffer vertigo when the markets tip. She is in corporate events and promotes a chain of conference centers; suffers from migraines when prospective suppliers reject her request for confidential commissions. Their children are at expensive private schools - the boy is well liked, and has friends and does well at his studies, but his younger sister struggles with everything.

Both husband and wife are ambitious. To meet the expectations of their companies, they push themselves, gain promotion; seem successful and satisfied, altogether admirable. But, despite their high incomes, they are always paying something off, always in debt, and the pressure to perform causes much stress. And there are other factors that demand almost the same amount of time and attention: driving their children to and from school, to and from piano, karate and ballet lessons; driving them to and from friends; taking the daughter to a psychologist; shopping for all sorts of things at different malls. However, the most sapping of all, is that their aged parents are growing frail, prone to accidents and diseases - recently his father has been diagnosed with cancer, and her mother is showing more and more signs of senility. So they live day by day with rush hour traffic, blocked deals, presentations that fail and the burden of helping their parents cope financially and emotionally, trying not to be depressed by the old people's weakening minds and deteriorating bodies.

Then one Sunday evening, projecting ruefully to the week that lies ahead, they decide to take a trip, get away. And within a week they arrange for someone to look after their children while they fly to an oasis in the middle of a desert.

*

The oasis has long been the site of luxurious hostelries catering for the elites that dominated the political and economic lives of various empires. It is a rare and striking profusion of natural and human wealth; lush groves of trees and terraced gardens slope away from luxurious residences and trading arcades. The oasis has always been a place of contention; every generation has seen clashes between local tribes and invading armies. In the course of its long history it has been heavily fortified; its walls have a single entry - an iron gate decorated with lions and falcons. The most recent conqueror had been particularly lavish and fitted the hostelries with sublime and original sensitivity. Now, in this globalised time, the oasis has become a highly desired tourist destination, an unusually romantic location offering the very wealthy superior taste and delight.

*

They cross the desert in a specially designed vehicle and arrive at dusk. The battlements are cloaked in subtle light. They ring the great bell that hangs in front of the gate, then drive into a courtyard studded with statues and giant palms. They tip the porters generously to find their room is furnished as it was in the times of the princes and merchants, the soldiers and civil servants of past centuries.

The desert beyond the ramparts is a deep dark blue. The stars that fill the sky are many and splendid, infinite, unlike the cosmic isolation experienced in their brightly lit city. They walk in the garden, sit awhile by a fountain. Listening to the lapping of the water, they inhale the aromatic perfume exuded by date palms. Afterwards, their embrace is a lingering and hungry one. They make love in the bath. Then they make love in the four-poster bed. And their lovemaking is so pleasurable, so intense, so free, that it is as if they have refashioned their bodies, rewritten the adorations of their beginning.

They go down to dinner. In the intimacy of interlocking chambers, a trio of musicians plays ancient instruments. The waiters, who wear subtly woven robes, are obliging and efficient. They order from an astoundingly varied menu. The food is superb. Later they stroll again in the garden. Other couples pass them in the half-dark. The air is filled with low murmurings. Smoothed and scented by silk sheets, they make love again. Then they sleep, wonderfully complete, at peace in each other's arms.

The following day they ride out into the desert. Caves with chiseled inscriptions and stone age drawings are to be found in nearby hills. They climb to the summit of a granite mound; the quiet vastness of the desert surrounds them. That night, on their return to the oasis, they eat at a restaurant by a pool. Another group of musicians plays. After the meal they are again consumed by desire.

The week passes. They must return to the city.

Every night they have phoned their children and their parents. Their conversations have been short, but filled with love and concern. Indeed, they have spoken with calmness, without resentment or anxiety. But now they feel apprehension, even dread: can they preserve the freshness and beauty of the oasis?

Will they?

*

As they step back into the house, their daughter rushes out crying - her sports bag has been stolen at school, the teachers have ignored her; the other girls have called her a slut because she wears short skirts. Their son smiles; he hugs them, shows them his excellent mark for maths.

The house is tidy. The smell of food drifts from the kitchen - the domestic has handled everything well. The telephone rings and he takes it. His mother has just had a heart attack but is stabilizing.

The sky is filled with the sound of an aircraft; a dog barks.

*

The next day, returning to rush hour traffic, they find the streetlights aren't working. The newspaper headlines announce that the interest rate on home bonds has risen by fifteen percent; a new corruption scandal has hit the ruling party; a major corporation has been liquidated; the government is retrenching thousands of workers; a deadly new virus has broken out in the south; civil war has erupted in a major energy producing country.

That evening they decide to plant a palm tree in their garden. Then they leave the children and go shopping for a four-poster bed and bags of fine sand. When they return home, they find their children asleep. On the kitchen table is a note in the boy's handwriting:

Hope you found what you were looking for. Me and little sis couldn't wait to see the two of you chill out. Before you hit the desert you were both so crabby. But when you came back you were cool. Stay that way, mom and dad. Stay that way. After all, we didn't make the world the way it is.

Love,

De kidz

ps   if you need help carrying the bed, wake me.

HURRY

L ate afternoon; a train reaches its last station. A man alights. He
carries a heavy suitcase packed with precious things.

He leaves the station, hurries home along the muddy path that
runs beside a winding stream. He rushes along, gripping the suitcase
handle tightly. How happy everyone will be when he arrives! How
happy he will be!

He walks fast, sweating because of the weight and his eagerness.
He thinks he is making good time. But the suitcase has a tear that he
does not know about, a tear that widens with each stride. His pre-
cious things slip out onto the mud. One by one, they fall. Only when
the suitcase is empty does he realize what has happened.

It is almost dark. He can barely see. He runs back to gather his
precious things, searches for them everywhere, looks frantically un-
der rocks and bushes. And he finds them all, and cleans them; rubs
off the last traces of mud, the last vestiges of dullness. How lucky he
was to have retrieved them! How relieved he feels! Then stitching up
the suitcase (so that it is once more whole and strong), he repacks
his precious things, and sets off again along the winding path by the
stream.

To keep up his spirits he begins talking aloud. Surely nothing fur-
ther can delay him! He redoubles his pace to make up for lost time,
but the suitcase weighs him down, and the winding path seems to
stretch on forever. Suddenly the suitcase again tears open; his pre-
cious things fall out onto the mud.

The suitcase is useless! He flings it down. It will never hold his
precious things securely.

The precious things disappear. One by one, he watches them sink. He stares as the last treasure passes from sight. Then he walks off. But this time he sings - empty hands, swinging. And he does not look back. Stepping lightly, he is at last at home on the muddy path by the winding stream.

THE INTERSECTION

Active hands, eternal in a mutual, life-giving exchange.

Every Friday Abel goes shopping to the same mall, buys food and other supplies for the weekend. He buys staples and the odd luxury, the odd treat, the odd present for his wife and children and for himself. And every Friday he takes the same route home; and this means stopping at the intersection of Houghton Drive and Louis Botha Avenue. Now he always stops because, without fail, the robots are red. And while he waits for the lights to change, he is always greeted by a young man.

This man sells vegetables and toys, and other seasonal needs. He sells to drivers as they wait for the lights to change. No matter the weather he sells; every day, hour after hour, moving up and down the traffic. And though he is sometimes joined by other sellers, the work is demanding - the petrol fumes, the noise, the incessant coming and going of vehicles - and they soon fade away. So the intersection becomes his turf, his spot. And he is thankful for the other sellers' inconsistency, their inability to handle the pressure, for he depends on it: he, his mother and his young woman and their child. They all come to depend on this intersection - and the red light that forces the drivers to stop, and the smile on his face that opens the windows and then their pockets.

So Abel knows the young man and from time to time buys from him. And one Friday he buys a box of avocados. And because the price (as usual) is reasonable, far lower than the supermarkets, and the quality is high, Abel smiles, and thanks the young man. The young man thanks him in turn and then, quite unexpectedly, hands Abel a piece of paper. And Abel, hearing hooting behind him, drives off without being able to ask why he has given it to him or what it's about.

The paper lies on the seat on top of the avocados; folded in half, quite crumpled - a small piece of dirty, white paper that covers a green fruit. Abel pulls over to the side of the road, and reads: *Next Friday you will buy two bags from me. The next Friday you will buy three. The next, four. And so it will be - every week you will buy an extra bag till I cannot get enough bags to satisfy you. By that time I will be a rich man. Thank you, my brother. I will never forget your kindness.*

Abel chuckles all the way home. The next Friday when he sees the young man he asks for two bags. The young man sells him two. He drives home. Who will believe him? The previous week's bag has still not been eaten – and the family is growing tired of avocado. And now he has bought two more bags. But when his wife sees the two bags, she joins in his laughter and praises the power of the seller. And the children make jokes about *avo-stew* and *avo-pie* and *avo-omelette*. Abel slices open the last two of the previous week's bag and prepares a salad with egg and onion. Then he makes some toast.

The next week he buys three bags, the next four and the next five. He buys, and buys, always smiling. The fruit pile up till the house is full of rotting bags and his family's amusement turns to disdain: the children become morose, his wife turns into a shrew. Week after week he buys; the young man ready with the bags on the pavement, loading them quickly enough not to block up the traffic. But eventually a Friday comes when Abel stops at the intersection, the robot stays red, and the young man rushes up to him sweating with a trolley bearing thirty-four bags of avocados, and Abel leans out the window and says, "Enough! Sorry, but enough! I can't take anymore, I can't! No room, my friend! No room, absolutely no room!" Then feeling strangely defensive, he prepares to accelerate. But the young man does not seem disappointed. He rushes to the side of the road, grabs a piece of paper and a pen from a battered bag and scribbles furiously. Then he runs back to Abel and passes him this note and, as usual, waves good-bye when the lights change.

Abel drives off, feeling quite guilty - the young man must surely be angry. And curious as to what he has written, he pulls over as soon as the traffic allows. But before reading the note, he reflects that, in fact, the young man has no justification to feel aggrieved: for weeks now, he has made good money. And that being the case, he, Abel, can feel good, knowing that he has done good, and that whatever the temporary annoyance, his family will recover their good spirits once they see that the flow of bags has stopped, and will soon look back on this episode as a great adventure.

Abel reads: *There is too much fruit in your house. You have no where to pack it. Your family is unwelcoming. You feel a fool. Your wife throws all the fruit into a giant pot. And the more you bring, the more she throws into the pot. Then the fruit stands for many days till you smell its juicy smell and you look down into the pot. There is a pool of golden liquid. You sip this liquid and the taste is unlike anything you have ever tasted. And you bottle this liquid, and offer it to your neighbour, who tastes it and asks for more, and you make more, but this time you sell it to him and soon you cannot keep up with his orders and you become a rich man. Thank me, thank me, my brother.*

*

Abel shows the note to his wife. The next day he buys a giant container. That Friday he finds the young man at the intersection with a trolley of thirty-six bags of avocados, and he buys all thirty-six and drives home, and chops up the avocados and throws them into the giant container.

The next week he buys thirty-nine bags and throws them into the container; the next, forty, and the next, forty-seven; till the perfume rising from the container makes him giddy, and peering over the edge he sees a syrup of the deepest, most alluring green-gold. And when he samples it, he is delirious with pleasure. He offers a jar to his neighbour. The neighbour is very satisfied and asks for more. Abel is pleased to give him another jar. The next day the neighbour pleads for another and this time Abel sells him another, then another, and another, till Abel is unable to keep up with the demand because the neighbour buys so many jars.

Then others in the neighbourhood hear about it and buy, and soon everyone is ordering jars and he is a rich man. And though new producers eventually enter the market, Abel and the man at the intersection stay rich; and years later their children, who all become executives in the avocado syrup company, erect a memorial stone at the intersection of Nelson Mandela Drive and Oliver Tambo Avenue (the new names for Houghton Drive and Louis Botha Avenue). On top of the marble block they place a sculpture: two green/golden hands - one offering a box of avocados, the other outstretched to receive it.

THE SLEEPING MAN

The man was sleeping heavily. Suddenly he woke, and sat up. His wife continued sleeping beside him. He could not see the clock, just heard its ticking. Without disturbing her, he eased out of bed and began dressing. Once he had finished dressing, he gently closed the bedroom door behind him. He heard the dogs stir outside, but they did not bark when he slipped into the garage and started the car. He drove off.

The moon was still high and he felt very calm. He drove fast; there were no other cars. The city was heavy with rain that had fallen earlier in the evening. He opened the windows to allow the coolness to wash over him, swallowed the sleep saliva clogging his mouth. Then, once he reached a certain neighborhood, he stopped the car and checked his pockets. He counted the money, turned into a darkened street.

A woman was standing alone on a street corner. She was dressed in a short skirt; her mouth was made up with purple lipstick. She smiled to him as he pulled over and lowered his window. But she did not speak, just opened the door and climbed in. Then, while he was driving, she began to fondle him. His penis grew stiff. She bent over him, slipped on a condom, and took his penis in her mouth. He cupped her breasts and buttocks and quickly reached orgasm. She removed the clouded condom. But as she began rolling down the window to throw it out into the street, he took the condom from her, and placed it in a plastic bag under his seat. Then he drove back to the place where he had picked her up. As they reached the corner, he dipped into his back pocket and offered her a few notes. They said good-bye to one another. She called him 'sweetie'.

At the next corner he saw another woman in a short skirt. She wore green lipstick. As he slowed down, she lifted her skimpy top and exposed her breasts. Once in the car beside him, she began to caress his penis. Then, she, too, began to kiss and suck him. He came, removed the condom and placed it in the same plastic bag. Then he drove her back to the street corner, and paid her.

At the third intersection a woman in a short skirt with gunmetal lipstick smiled at him. She danced forward, massaging herself between the legs. He ignored her. But when a few minutes later he passed another woman performing the same routine, he turned back, and picked up the first. She was sweaty, stale, with cracked eyes. But she knew what he wanted. Once again he stashed the used condom in the plastic bag, felt in his back pocket for money, and dropped her off.

The first signs of dawn were streaking the dark city. He switched on the radio. There was music but he did not hear the music. When he reached home, the dogs greeted him with loud barks and sniffed at his hands. He parked the car and took out the plastic bag. He walked over to the garden shed, took a spade, dug a hole at the far end of the garden, and buried the plastic bag. Then he washed his hands.

He entered the bedroom, undressed. His wife rolled over as he slipped into bed. He kissed her, and she curled up to him. He lay quietly as her breathing settled. Then he lay holding her breasts until he too fell asleep. Outside the dogs were digging up the plastic bag. They carried it over to the place at the opposite end of the garden where they reburied the bags he brought back every night.

When the man woke for work, the daylight made his eyes blink and the black garden soil showed trails of milky silver; the compulsive oozing of a cruising snail, the sticky strands of an unmoored spider web.

PLATO'S COACH

H e is the coach of a soccer team. His son is the star player in another team. These two teams play in the same league, so from time to time, they play each other. How does the father feel? Which team does he want to win?

When Socrates's son, Plato, sketched this situation and set him these questions, Socrates thought for some time, then replied,

In every situation we seek harmony and beneficial outcomes. But there are inevitably clashes of interest. That being the case, subtlety is required in order to provide the fairest and most appropriate response to the situation you have described. May I be equal to the task, my son!

Socrates paused as his son laughed.

Get on with it, dad!

And Socrates gave him a hug.

But let me start with another question: what is the function of a coach?

Plato answered, To train a team.

And what does that mean?

To teach a team so that they play better.

Better?

That they improve so that they win.

And what if they lose?

We will say the coach no good

So winning is a key sign of success?

Yes.

Even if the victory is achieved through fouls and unattractive, dull play or just simple luck?

No, of course not!

Skill, panache . . .

Yes! That's what counts, but . . . it's still better to win than to lose!

They both laugh. Socrates smiles and touches his son's cheek.

Much better to win than to lose, but better to lose honorably than to win by foul means.

Stop preaching, dad, says Plato, I know all this stuff!

Socrates puts on a funny voice and says, I should bloody well hope so.

Get back to the point, says Plato.

Socrates scratches his belly.

You look at things over time – not just one match. You look at the overall picture. Right? Now let's move on. As a father, what's special about your relationship with your son?

You love him.

Why?

Because he's your child.

And what if he does bad things to other people?

Then you feel ashamed.

Aha! You feel bad – for him and for the one who was on the wrong end of his bad deed. And you feel bad because you want him to do well, in fact, to excel. If he does that, it's a good thing for him, but also for you as his father. And if his team does well, that also encourages you, gives you a sense of pride.

Of course, dad.

And if he is the star of the team, so much the better?

Obviously!

So what happens if his team wins the match through his last minute goal . . . but you see the goal was scored through a foul, or through an offside position? How will you feel?

Disappointed.

Why?

Because he did not score it fairly, the win was a fake.

Exactly! And how do you deal with this?

You tell your son you're upset that he fouled another player and that his victory is not something to be proud of.

And what do you say to your team about your son's behaviour?

You say nothing unless they ask you.

And if they do ask you?

You tell them what you feel – that you're disappointed in him.

Disappointed. Hmm, not a nice feeling. And is it easy to share your disappointment with others?

No.

Why?

Because it's painful to you that he has done a bad thing. And as you said, it also makes you look bad.

Socrates and his son stand silent for a moment digesting this double blow.

Then his son continues, It's like you didn't teach him properly.

And is that fair?

No. He isn't your robot! He makes his own decisions, acts the way he wants to even if you taught him in a certain way.

So you would tell your team that you are disappointed in your own son.

Yes.

Yes, you would and that's a tough decision. You would be a very brave father. Now what happens if your son scores a last minute goal against your team? A match winning goal that is entirely fair. In fact, an act of brilliance.

You will be very happy for your son but sad for your team.

Yes, it will be wonderful to see your son stand out for excellence, but a bit sad to see your team lose. After all, you've invested so much in them, and all that time and effort counts for nothing at the last moment because of him. But what will you feel if it's the other way round? Your team wins because of a bad mistake made by your son. Let's say through an own goal, or through giving away a penalty. Makes you shiver, doesn't it?

Ja . . . that's a tough one!

What do you say to him and what do you say to your team?

You tell him to try harder – if it was a simple mistake. Or you tell him to stop being stupid and reckless if he caused a foul. Of course, if it was clearly bad luck, you encourage him to keep up his spirits. I mean, bad luck strikes each and every one of us at some time or another.

Yes, my boy, it certainly does! Now here's another scenario: he played brilliantly but his team still lost despite the fact that your team played poorly.

You mean his team was unlucky to lose?

Exactly!

You tell him to keep up the good work and you scold your team for playing badly.

But which was more important - his brilliance or your team's failure?

Both. You have to deal with both aspects, work at both levels.

And do you give your son tips how to play against your team?

Of course not!

But why not? You love him. You want him to shine!

Yes, you love him more than any other boy in the two teams but you can't be seen to favour him – certainly not at the expense of the team you coach.

Even though blood is thicker than water?

You mean money!

Ha, ha! No, you're right - you get paid to coach the team but not to father a child.

Like hell you don't! Kids have to support you guys when you're old!

Socrates laughs, Are you up for that, my boy? Well, I hope so! But just to conclude: as coach you know the money part isn't the most important - you want the satisfaction of seeing your team play well and preferably winning.

Boring . . . that's what you said right at the beginning, dad.

Ok, ok. Just reminding you, son.

Plato puts his arm round his father and winks.

So that settles it. Now we know what to do about the match on Saturday. But still, dad, how you going to handle me scoring the winning goal against your chumps?

TRAINS, BUILDINGS, BIRDS AND PIGS

I am walking on a narrow, broken path. Many people are rushing along the same path but at different speeds; no one talks and none of us knows where we are going although in the distance we can see a city. My brother comes up behind me. I am overjoyed to see him, but he, too, does not walk with me. He runs past, overtaking me by stepping onto the even more rutted and obstacle-strewn wasteland that runs alongside the path. I try to keep up with him. But I cannot.

Ahead of us I see a railway line. Then I hear a loud rushing noise - a train is bearing down towards us. It is an old train. The compartments are slightly shabby, but comfortable; the seats covered with deep, soft upholstery. At first sight I envy the passengers on the train - they are all young, healthy-looking men and women. But on closer observation I note that they ignore one another, exist separate and remote.

Suddenly my brother runs towards the railway line. He darts forward in front of the train. I jerk back in horror. He will be crushed under the giant wheels! But when I look up, I see that he has crossed the lines safely. Relieved, I resume my walk, still puzzled by his dangerous behaviour, but secretly saluting his courage and skill. However, my jubilation is short-lived. I see another railway line beyond the first; another train is steaming down it at even greater speed. My brother again rushes forward. Paralyzed by fear, I watch him try to beat this second train. I shout out. My vision blurs. Hooting loudly, the train sweeps by. I look up. My brother has once more achieved the impossible! There he is, safe, on the far side of the tracks. I want to embrace him, but to my disappointment, he disappears from sight.

I continue walking; I cross the lines. The stream of people now leaves the dirt path and surges towards the city. The momentum is unstoppable. I look around. Away from the railway lines are old buildings that remind me of Central Europe. They are decayed but stylish, and still retain a sense of elegance, of restrained, if complex design. Then it occurs to me that I have seen similar buildings in the Middle East. But as I step along, passing one building after another, I realize that I am in Africa and that the task before us is to rebuild and renovate these buildings, restore and enhance them, so that they transcend their past impressiveness, past attractiveness.

I walk on, wondering if I will meet my brother. People begin to peel away from the crowd and enter the buildings. I am curious. What are they going to be doing in the buildings? What tasks are theirs? But I remain in the dark. There are no notice boards identifying the names and professional spheres of the companies occupying each one. Meanwhile I stroll down a wide boulevard. Then I, too, walk into one of the buildings. Inside I am not sure what is more prevalent, the old or the refurbished, but I see from those in the foyer that there is purposefulness and energy, projecting a pulsating future. And I am heartened. Though I do not find my brother I am impressed and begin to feel secure.

*

Some time later my partner and I are driving on a highway that runs beside the ocean. Above us a flock of white birds fly in formation. The sight is so organized, yet spontaneous, that we stop the car to admire their unity, their cohesion. The birds beat their wings effortlessly, glide with the air currents, all the while keeping a distance from one another though seeming to be one giant organism. What an inspiring, restorative sight! At last, a simple, spontaneous activity free of doubt or worry or deliberation!

Then, when we turn inland and leave the ocean, behind fences, divided up into different compounds, I see small herds of mottled, black/white pigs run forward towards the gates. At the gates are their keepers. It is feeding time. In the keepers hands are bones - bones that are usually given to dogs. I become very angry. Why are these ugly little pigs being given dog food? This makes no sense. Pigs eat offal, not nutritious, tasty bones!

DETERMINED LOVE

He is highly aroused by her. He stalks her at parties. She resists him at first, but he is insistent. She lies to him about where she works. He tracks her down. She agrees to go out with him, and later that evening, on the carpet of her flat, they make love. In the weeks that follow, they sleep together every night and she, too, becomes besotted with him. Joined in their mutual desire, the world breathes sweetly, becomes bigger.

She proposes they live together. He agrees; he buys a house. They make this house their own special place. Their lives run on, their bond becomes stronger. Then she falls pregnant. They accept the child gladly. But after a few weeks she suffers a miscarriage, and her recovery is complicated. He nurses her. Week after week he gives up everything to ease her sorrow, retreats from the world to attend to her needs. And when she recovers and is able to enjoy living again, he is ecstatic. But they cannot have sex - it causes her too much pain.

He accepts what the doctors say will be temporary abstention. Though she tries to satisfy him in different ways, he hungers for love-making. Months pass. Despite his frustration, he shows understanding, gives unstinting attention. They spend all their time together: talking, listening to music, going for walks, but inevitably other realities come into focus: she has no real interests beyond the house, and few friends. And she has no money of her own, and knows nothing about managing money, so that he has to pay for everything and he fears that she expects him to support her forever.

There is tension, they fight. She fears he might start to see other women. Suppressing the pain, she forces herself to sleep with him. She falls pregnant again. Fearing for her health, he insists that she have an abortion, but the doctors advise that such a step might kill her. So she has the baby and they both love the child so much he cannot believe he had doubts. The child is their pride, the cement that keeps them strong. Then months later she has a relapse of the old problem, and though the pain returns with a vengeance, she forces herself to sleep with him till she hurts so bad, and is so ill, that she absolutely cannot have sex.

The months pass. He is frustrated, but in the cause of their love tries to revive his old patience and understanding. He takes over looking after the boy, throws himself into his work, joins a sports club; does all the conventional things a man can do. But he cannot fight his needs. She senses his restlessness, his looking elsewhere. Frightened that this time he really will go, embittered by her weakness, despite her knowing that she is being illogical, she rejects him; is short tempered, speaks foully. He reacts angrily though he knows why she does this (how can she be blamed for her body's failure?), but a part of him thinks she is doing this to spite him, and that she is happy because she has what she wants: whatever happens between them, she will have the house. So he pays for the memory of their ardour: he pays for staying loyal to her and their child; he pays with bitter nights of longing for the beautiful, soft tautness of women. And little by little, he concedes what his body knows: he has so much desire, but now, not for her; he so much needs to touch and caress women, but now, not her. And because he does not want to abandon her, and yet has no control over his fantasies, he laughs at, mocks, himself. And he refuses to leave the house.

They live in separate rooms. Outside in the world he flirts with whoever he likes; he courts ridicule. He sets up another woman in a flat, makes her his secret second wife. Solace and celebration; but passion, the cult of the moment and fantasy, can also bring death. At times he hates himself for needing women; hates himself for hating women for making him need them. He lies his way between the two until the new one kicks him out. He plans moving to another city, starting a new life. But then he suddenly feels depressed, deflated, everything seems to be dark and futile.

He reaches a point where his depression is so great that he cannot work. The bills pile up. The rates and the electricity must be paid, and food bought, and their child looked after. He lies in bed, day after day, unwashed, half-dead and desperate. And now she, his first love who had cut him off but could not be blamed, manages to find the strength to go out and work. She reverses the roles: supports him, gives him an allowance. And given this chance to dig so deep that there is nothing left to come out, he stabilizes, starts to respect her again though part of him resents her sudden recovery. Why could she not have done this long ago? But after a while he, too, feels better till he is strong enough to fetch the child from school and do the shopping.

Driving around the neighbourhood he watches the passing women. He feels ashamed to be lusting in front of his young child, but he cannot hold back; he so much desires their unknown bodies. And all this time she keeps working - while sensing his turmoil, his longing. For she still cannot have sex; something in her has died. And she pities him, but because she loves him, she does not attack him for disappearing at night. And slowly, in the depths of her calm, her support, his distractions subside. They agree to again share a bed. They are tender to each other. But through an unspoken yet absolute agreement, they never try to make love. Satisfied to hold each other every night before turning to their separate sides, they live together until their deaths: a man and a woman who shared much in the way of experience.

THE DEFILED SANCTUARY

He refuses to allow them to drain the pure energy the transformation of the ruined house has given him.

Walking about on a sparsely populated island, Abel arrives at a secluded beach. He strolls on the white sand, lets the cold tingle of the waves excite him. Then he crosses a clump of rocks and on the far side finds an abandoned house.

In the hollowed, blackened corners of each room are indentations; they seem to be niches, prayer niches, where figurines stood and candles and incense were burnt. Outside is a wild garden. Here he comes across altar-like fireplaces where religious ceremonies were possibly practiced. Though there are no physical remains or artifacts relating to rituals, there are traces, smears, of unidentifiable substances which suggest them. And Abel walks through the house thinking about these intimations of worship. What forms did they take? What inspired them? And who were the congregants and why have they disappeared and left this empty shell? He looks about him, sits down on the dirty floor. And suddenly the dim-lit interior frightens him. Will it not be advisable to go back outside? The sun is shining and the beach is idyllic. Why stay in this foul-smelling ruin? And the longer he sits, the stronger his intuition that evil ceremonies took place; ceremonies for summoning powers that defile and destroy. A shudder passes through him. And yet he does not leave; something very powerful holds him.

Abel rises, begins clearing the debris. He washes down a ledge that has traces of blood; he mutates drawings of distorted, malevolent forms that line the walls into symbols of vitality and harmony; he perfumes all areas imbued with stench. All day he busies himself in this task of purification, cleansing the house and the garden. And while he works, he feels uplifted. And at sunset, he is proud to see that the house is transformed - is now truly worthy of being a sacred place. Rooted to the earth, he feels its outer radiance and his inner sense of accomplishment fuse. But as the two reach their climax, a group of silent, blank-faced people enter the house and surround him.

The crowd grows, and he is, at first, welcoming of their presence. Despite their dourness, they will surely also experience his joy at the reconsecrated temple! But when they insist on facing away from him, and refuse to greet him, he is disquieted. Why this hostile indifference? Why are they so bent on denying his existence? Is it possible that they are offended by his holy work? Then the people slowly pack around him, casting out their anger. But Abel forces himself to regard them without fear. He tells himself that despite this rejection of him, they will be won over; once they realize that a far more powerful and true god now inhabits the house, these misguided people will be devoted to noble and uplifting causes. So he decides to address them. But as he is about to speak, two arms clamp him from behind;

Gripped tight, unable to move, a giant shadow towers above him; the faceless crowd projects its hate. But no voice explains why he is being held, no sign is given as to why he has been seized. The vice-like arms do not let up for a moment. As much as he struggles, Abel is utterly at their mercy. And he realizes that the giant is not simply possessed of great physical strength - he is surely the high priest of this satanic group, this temple which cleansing has perversely defiled. And filled with this knowledge Abel stops resisting: no matter his efforts, the house will again be polluted, the corrupt congregation has returned to claim it.

The crowd pushes closer; the giant's grip is relentless. But then, suppressing despair, Abel breathes deeply, relaxes. He understands that though he will not be able to break free, he does not have to surrender his joy at having had the honour of being the instrument of restoration - no matter how short-lived this triumph, that privilege can never be taken from him.

He stands proudly though held prisoner, and all about him the house vibrates with the integrity of his efforts, the strength of his commitment.

WHITE MAGIC

Taking fruit is strictly forbidden, but our diet is so bland, devoid of taste and nutritional value, and I am determined to change my life.

I am a prisoner in a labour camp. The camp is hidden inside a hollow mountain. Cut off from the world, a vast workforce shuffles wearily, labouring in a perpetual twilight. A merciless, omnipotent taskmaster controls us.

We operate a production line, canning fruit and vegetables. As the cans are processed, we pack them in boxes for distribution to unknown destinations. It is strictly forbidden to eat of the foodstuffs we are packing, and hungry as we are, none of us dare disobey this rule for the penalty is death. I have no special rights. But though I am very conscious of the masses and their servitude, and think constantly about how to oppose this condition, I feel set apart knowing that they are too fearful and broken in spirit to join me in revolt.

Then, one day, while the taskmaster is not looking, I select a tin of fruit from the conveyor belt, and hide it in my overall. I climb a ladder. It leads to a small platform that is suspended over the cavern. From this viewpoint I look out at the production line: the conveyor belts, the prisoners, the tens of thousands of cans moving towards the packing section. And I feel victorious - I have defied the overseer. Even if they will not follow me, I have shown the others that it is possible to rebel.

I open the can, but before I can eat the fruit, the taskmaster sees me, and orders me down.

I feel my body flush with the danger, but I leave the platform and approach the taskmaster. He holds out his hand. The prisoners barely look up; the outcome of defiance is obvious. But I do not panic. With springing steps I reach the taskmaster and calmly pass him the can. Then I wait for the punishment.

*

It is a bright, blue, winter day. The air is cold and fresh. I am on the slope near the hollow mountain. The snow is very thick, packed hard into ice. Though free, I am troubled, oppressed by this isolation. Knowing that the work camp with its enslaved masses is inside the mountain, preoccupies me, unsettles me.

I scan the slopes. A white creature comes into view. It has two large antlers; its flanks are thick with shaggy hair. Despite its gross hide, it moves with perfect grace, almost flying over the snow. Dazzled, I absorb its strength and vitality - this creature, poised and light, bewilderingly familiar yet unknown and unearthly.

I stand on the slope entranced by this white magic. Then I decide, no matter the difficulty, no matter the price, to find a way into the hollow mountain and confront the taskmaster. But, before I can act, the creature begins to race towards the mound.

The spectacle of its power and speed is breathtaking. I watch it reach the cliff face. Then, as it touches the mountain, there is a tremendous explosion and the rock is peeled open, the factory destroyed. The mass of prisoners stand incredulous. How could the great cavern have been ripped open? The confines of their miserable lives suddenly lifted so that at long last they feel the liberating rays of the sun!

I watch as they pour out of the labour camp. The slopes are filled with shouting, crying men and women. And I, too, speak out words of thanks, of consolation: in my hand, once again, is the can of sweet fruit.

AHEAD

"Peaceful madmen are ahead of the future"   *Gabriel Garcia Marquez*

A bel is at a party. Men and women dance; all about laughing dancers, whirling dancers. But Abel stands to the side. He feels the beat, the pulse of the drums and bass, the flight of the flute, yet he does not move. He stands alone at the edge of the dance floor, and watches; he watches the faces, the arms, the thighs, the feet. And he smiles.

On the other side of the dance floor are two men, two rough, shaven-headed men with thick bodies. These men also stand, watching at the edge. And Abel knows that these men are preparing themselves, readying themselves, but not for the dance – the two men are preparing themselves for a journey into the world beneath the coordinated flow, the rhythm; the world beneath the music of the dance.

And he knows that they have sensitized themselves, conditioned themselves for a journey that many have intended, and in fact, upon which many have embarked, but from which few have returned; they are about to enter a dimension without borders, one with contradictory signs and hazily known laws. And knowing this, he wonders why they still stand at the side of the dance floor observing the desperate shaking of limbs, the smiles and winks, rubbing up of body against body, the fondling, the excitement . . . For the two men smile with a measure of pity watching the crowd, they smile with a degree of indulgence. How sad and predictable that the ignorant drown themselves in cheap, superficial pleasures from which they soon grow tired, and for which they inevitably have to seek fresh partners.

169

Abel knows the two men have the knowledge of those prepared to be totally possessed, as the lucid madness that cannot bear the false-ness and disappointment of the world will rage in them, and then transport them beyond rage as they taste freedom from the fear of death. And to this end they have been in training; they have studied the special texts, the codes, the manuscripts composed by others who turned away from the dance floor, and embarked upon this journey, and who did in fact return with new fire; a fire that consumes but restores itself, endlessly renewing. So Abel watches them with a mix-ture of suspicion (do they think themselves superior?) and affection (he does not have past memories of a shared childhood but somehow he knows them as intimately as if they had grown up together).

Then he realizes that they are his brothers, indeed, his twin broth-ers. No! One is his sister! And Abel is pleased to note this. It is good to have both a brother and a sister. He watches his brother and sister across the jiving bodies, the lustful eyes darting from figure to figure. And then, without warning, he feels himself drawn onto the dance floor (was he pulled or did he slip?), feels the heat of the bodies around him, the flurry, the pulse, the strong perfume of sweat and alcohol and flowery scents almost suffocating him. He becomes part of the kissing and the groping, the sighs and the groans of pleasure. And as he sees his brother and sister also pulled in, consumed by the groove, he feels himself going under, drowning with these vibrating, unthinking, quite blind, but joyful bodies.

Abel throws up his arms, cries out. Will they survive? Will they withstand the torrent of desire? Will their hours and days and years of training and meditation enable them to hold their heads above the rush, the current? But then, though he hears syrupy voices propose means of rescue, he feels himself relax, at peace. The clamminess is gone; his body is cool and fresh. His brother and sister seem simi-larly composed. He sees the others, the masses of bodies gyrate, but though they are very close, it is as if they are at a distance. Everything is suspended and yet he is moving.

And so Abel, his brother and his sister, stand in the middle of the dance floor, hands clasped together, three motionless warriors danc-ing with perfect rhythm.

Printed in the United States
By Bookmasters